Campfire Reflections

Dr. Dale Linebaugh

Campfire Reflections

Dr. Dale Linebaugh
101 Rodeo Drive
Spring Creek, PA 16436
www.MiracleMountainRanch.org

Cover and interior design: Abigail Snyder

Table of Contents

Too Close to Home to Turn Back

The young hands are all full of questions,
as we sit by the fireside and chat,
They ask of the trails that I've ridden,
and the places and horses I've sat.

Their eyes seem to glow in the firelight,
and I know they are thinking of when
I was young, and as full of ambition,
as each of them seems to have been.

Tell how they ranched in the old days?
How far away was a town?
How did you start out a new horse?
How often did one put you down?

Were there thrills when you roped at a roundup?
Was your job to head or to heel?
When the branding was done and the herd was paired up,
tell us, sir, how did you feel?

Don't you wish you could do it all over?
Run down the rope to your calf?
Ride out the kinks of an old bronc,
swap tales with the cowhands and laugh?

What is it like to be old sir?
Your strength and your health is so gone.
The dreams are all ended, your body is tired,
you're through when the day is half done.

It took me a while of reflection,
'twas true that my youth was long past.
I needed more rest, my eyesight was dim,
my energy just didn't last.

But, I had all my children well married,
the best thing, they all served the Lord.
My grandchildren loved being with me,
we all loved just reading God's Word.

My wife was still walking beside me,
God gave us three meals every day,
Our house was paid for, our love was still strong,
we've been blessed in just every way.

Out in the field is my old horse.
He nickers each time I draw near.
We still ride a bit, and when on him I sit,
I never do feel any fear.

Would I want to do it all over?
No, there's nothing on earth that I lack.
My cup just runs over with joy from the Lord,
and I'm too close to home to turn back.

- Dr. Dale Linebaugh

In Gratitude

Thanks to the elders of Grace Bible Church in Mineral Point, Wisconsin, founders of the Cowboy Country Church. They believed that the messages spoken in the meetings needed to be printed so that they could be studied and read again for a longer lasting challenge. They believed the messages should be shared with an even greater audience. Thank you, men of God, for your faith and encouragement.

My wife Opal, has had such a large part in this, reading and reading again the early manuscripts. Her words of advice and encouragement kept the project going. Thanks for letting me interrupt your schedule so often, and the work you were doing, to "read the next page, please." It takes a lot of love to face such interruptions.

Doctor Lew Sterrett, with his wife, Doctor Melodie, our daughter, fully understand the way of the horse and the lives of the cowboy, the rancher, the horse lover. They too see the connection between these creatures of God and the way God uses His creation to make spiritual things clear and powerful in the life of the individual. Traveling nationwide with their ministry of Sermon on the Mount, they are seeing hundreds brought into a vital relationship with Christ. Thanks, for being sold out to God. Thanks for riding with me on this new trail.

Our son, Jonathan, with Debbie his wife, kept after me to write, to share. Being a pastor, "Jed" as he is known, understands the need for a relationship with Christ, and the need to get the message out to the greatest audience possible by the means God has given us. Thanks for encouraging me to keep writing when it would have been easier to quit.

Mary Davis, of the CS Cattle Company in Cimarron, N.M. has always, because of her own relationship with Christ, been a blessing to me. She added to that by reading the rough draft along with her husband, Warren, then sharing her corrections and suggestions. Her recommendation of the book is meaningful to me. Thanks Mary for your words of encouragement.

Gail Allen, rancher and preacher and friend, thanks to you for reading the manuscript. Gail too read the rough draft with his wife Millie and made excellent suggestions for wording and changes. Thanks to you all.

Thanks to Mike Morrow, another great rancher and pastor, already too busy, who took time to look over the manuscript and send me his comments. Mike is a great preacher in a rapidly growing church.

Above all, I am grateful to Jesus Christ for Whom it is a privilege to write. I have had the joy, scores of times, usually with others, meeting with Him around campfires. He was always there. The warmth we experienced was not only from the flames of burning wood, but also from the presence of this Holy Savior, the very Son of God. Thank You, Jesus.

About the Author

Dr. Dale, as folks call him, has been active in the ministry of Jesus Christ for over sixty years. God has used him in a variety of ways: pastor, evangelist, missionary, church planter, founder of two Christian youth ranches, and president of a Christian college.

At the age of eight, Dale rode his first pony. At the age of eighty he is still riding in Southwestern Wisconsin where God sent him to plant two new ministries, Grace Bible Church and Cowboy Country Church. This is horse country where opportunities arise to ride with local ranchers gathering and working cattle. He also rides and assists in directing the Iowa County 4-H Mounted Drill Team. He no longer starts and trains horses as he did for twenty years in his younger days, but he still loves to ride a quiet, well-broke horse.

Saved just before he was sixteen, he experienced the struggle of so many who long to move forward from a redeemed experience with Christ to a relational experience with Him. More than anything else, the times alone with Christ, early in the morning before daybreak, were the hours when the relationship began and developed. This was the time and experience God used to change and mold a life.

From those times of devotions and from the hours spent studying the Word of God, a lifetime of preaching and teaching was born and grew. Now in the latter years of his life a few of those lessons learned from God and shared with others are finally written down. May the Holy Spirit Who inspired them to begin with, now go on to use them in your heart and in your life. I would ask for no greater reward.

Dr. Dale and Miss Opal Linebaugh
November 2008

Introduction

Christ went to the mountains to be alone. On one particular occasion He took His disciples along. From them He chose twelve to be His Apostles. The record is in Mark 3:13,14. "And He goeth up into a mountain, and calleth unto Him whom He would: and they came unto him. And He ordained twelve, that they should be with Him, and that He might send them forth to preach."

There is such a personal impact in the phrases: "called to Him." "They came to Him." "That they might be with Him." Before His representatives ever went forth to minister, they were called into a relationship, into being with Him.

As a newborn child of God's, I longed for that personal relationship experienced by being alone with the Word of God, in prayer, just with Him. The best time for me would be in the morning, but I just could not get started. The longing led to a struggle. No matter how much I prayed for God to get me out of bed and into His presence, it never happened. I would ask God to get me up and He never did. I began to wonder if God was interested in a relationship with me. Then one day a guest speaker came to the church I attended. He made a statement during his presentation that was almost a quote from my mind, though we had never met and talked. He stated: "Some of you are praying for God to get you out of bed in the morning so you can have your devotions. Quit praying about it and just get up!" From that day on I did just that and have never stopped.

My devotional life has been the greatest part of my life ever since. This is the time I find fellowship, love and comfort. Here I find conviction and cleansing. In that place my tired and wounded spirit finds strength and encouragement to go on. Just from being with Him, with Christ Jesus. This is the necessary ingredient before we go out to live, to witness, or to preach.

Though my focus was on reading the Bible, I found blessing and direction also from the writings of other men and women of God as I started the journey of relationship. Since I was so helped by others, it is my desire that the Scriptures used here and the sharing of my Relationship with Christ might encourage and challenge your relationship with Him. This is the prayer of my heart for you as you read, that you might sense the very presence of Christ.

1 The God of the Second Chance

"Seek ye the Lord while He may be found, call ye upon Him while He is near: Let the wicked forsake his way, and the unrighteous man his thoughts: and let him return unto the Lord, and He will have mercy upon him; and to our God, for He will abundantly pardon."

We were at a rodeo in Chattanooga, Tennessee and enjoying the rides AFTER the rodeo. Two of our friends were riding that night. One of them came out of the chute on a saddle bronc who simply lined out down the arena at a dead run. The judges gave the cowboy a reride. The second man came out of the chute on a bull who stumbled and fell. Again, the judges gave the cowboy a reride. These were being carried out after the rodeo proper had ended. Each boy had a second chance to win the prize.

When God works on a heart, He brings conviction, if that leads to confession, God grants cleansing and the issue is closed. Satan, on the other hand, loves to face us with accusations and cause us to confess the same things over and over again – which we have already confessed to God and been granted His cleansing. If that doesn't work to get us depressed, Satan loves to taunt the individual with the thought that he has lost every opportunity to get right with God and now it is too late. He does not want us to understand that God is the God of the Second Chance.

Abraham found that out, though it took him a long time to understand it. When God first led him from his home country in Ur of the Chaldees, he made a bargain with his wife, Sarah, that she would tell everyone that she was his sister. This bargain was in order to save Abraham from being killed by someone who might want her for a wife due to her extreme beauty. He lied about her to the Egyptians and was granted a large dowry by the king for her. God protected Sarah by bringing plagues to the king and his household, making him understand the real truth [Genesis 12:10-20]. Abraham was rebuked and left with Sarah. He also left clinging to the lie, blocking God's work and will in his life. Twenty five years later he was in the land of the Philistines [Genesis 20:1-18].

Sarah, now twenty-five years older, was still able to win in a beauty contest and was noticed immediately by Abimelech, king of Gerar who sent and took her. God stepped in again and kept Sarah safe, causing Abimelech to see the truth. Abraham is rebuked, and confesses the aged plot to lie. He never lies again and God works to fulfill the promise to Abraham. God gave him a second chance.

The problem with Moses was completely different. He tried to do the work of God in the power of the flesh and not in the will and way of God. Raised at first by his mother, then in the household of Pharaoh by Pharaoh's daughter, at the age of forty he paid a visit to his Hebrew brothers and started down the trail the wrong way. Seeing a Hebrew being beaten by an Egyptian taskmaster, he killed the Egyptian and hid his body in the sand. He was going to deliver Israel HIS way. The next day, knowing the murder was known, he fled to save his life and became a shepherd for the next forty years in the land of Midian. At the end of that second forty year span in his life, God called to him from a burning bush, gave him a commission to go and bring Israel out of Egypt, GOD'S way [Exodus 2:11,12; 3:7-10]. He gave Moses a second chance. And the Exodus became a reality in the next forty years of his life.

Sometimes we just don't want to do God's will and find a way to get "excused." Jonah's way was to pay for a ticket and head to Tarsus on a boat. God didn't buy his excuse and followed him up with a severe storm. Before the storm ended, Jonah confessed his sin to the sailors, was tossed in the sea, and swallowed by a large fish. Very possibly a whale. God did not say so. The third chapter of the book of Jonah begins with the words: "And the word of the Lord came to Jonah the second time, saying 'Arise, go unto Nineveh,...'" And Jonah went. God blessed and redemption and revival came to that wicked city. It is so very easy to reject and get out of God's will for your life. God is still willing to give you a second chance to get back in and get busy. Your greatest blessings may be just ahead of you.

Perhaps the two who mean so much to me In this matter are Peter and John Mark. I recall how Peter bragged that he would never deny the Lord, willing even to die for Him, yet he denied Him with profanity three times [Mark 14:66-72]. Mark, in a similar way, though without the profanity and vocal denial, turned his back on the work of the Lord and left the ministry he had shared with Barnabas and Paul. I can almost excuse him because he was evidently frightened out by the sudden involvement of spiritual warfare as Satan fought the ministry the three had. Nevertheless, he ran back home, even as Peter had "followed afar off." [Acts 13:6-13].

God dealt with Peter in a single sentence when an angel told the women at the tomb: "But go your way, tell His disciples and Peter that He goeth before you..." [Mark 16:7]. And Peter, what a wonderful addition to the commission. Peter was still included, God was giving him a second chance. John Mark had a second chance as Barnabas took him on a mission trip, right back to where he had left them, and got him back into service. In Paul's last epistle he made the statement to Timothy: "Take Mark and bring him with thee, for he is profitable to me for the ministry." [II Timothy 4:11]. Even here, a second chance.

The love of God was still there, the commission was still valid. And it is so for you today. Turn to the "God of the second chance," and begin anew the life and ministry God wants you to have.

2 Total Commitment

Paul had written to Timothy: "For the which cause I also suffer these things: nevertheless I am not ashamed: for I know Whom I have believed, and am persuaded that He is able to keep that which I have committed unto Him against that day." [II Timothy 1:12]. Committed, total commitment. What does that mean and how does it start?

Opal (my wife) and I were at the Iowa County High School Rodeo in Mineral Point, Wisconsin (yep, they've got some great ranches, cowboys and cowgirls in this Northern State) and enjoying it fully. Somehow as I watched, it dawned on me that there was a central theme exhibited here that I had seen numerous times in rodeos of past years, and yet had never really "seen." Whether it was riding a bronc or a bull, or coming out of the box to rope a calf or to head and heel a steer, there was a moment in each ride which was always identical. The moment of Total Commitment. And it always began the same way, with a nod of the head. The rider would get down on his bronc or his bull; or, the roper would back his horse into the box, ready to rope, then just nod! Total commitment was NOW. And there was no backing out. You were IN.

And why do they do it? For the adrenaline rush, a moment of fame, a new world record, a belt buckle or saddle, finances? Maybe to win a new trailer. The reasons vary, the commitment is identical.

I recalled that there were desires in the Christian's life as well. Primarily, we are to bring glory to God. For ourselves, there are some crowns that God makes available to us.

The Imperishable Crown [I Corinthians 9:25]. A Crown of Joy [I Thessalonians 2:19]. The Crown of Righteousness [II Timothy 4:8]. A Crown of Life [James 1:12]. And, a Crown of Glory [I Peter 5:4]. Those are all better than being King of the Cowboys or Miss Rodeo America, because those are crowns that last for eternity. They also bring glory to God as we will one day lay them at Jesus' feet.

Along with those desires, each cowboy and cowgirl, accepts that fact that there will also be some measure of grief. When one rides that competitively, it is not a matter of IF you get hurt, but WHEN, and how badly. In this one High School rodeo we witnessed a horse falling at the third barrel in barrel racing. A high school lad getting really messed up by a goat he was trying to tie down, a horse pulling back at the gate and breaking things up. And, of course, some whose only pay was a mouthful of dirt when they hit the ground.

Paul wrote that he suffered the loss of all things, to win Christ, and to really know Him [Philippians 3:18]. He warned us as well that all who lived godly in Christ Jesus would suffer [II Timothy 3:12,13]. And Peter added that we should not think it a strange thing to suffer if we live for Christ [I Peter 4:12]. Nope, if you rodeo, you are going to get hurt to some degree. And if you live for Christ, you will experience the cross in your own life. I don't know why we seem so surprised when it happens.

When a man (or woman) is down, how quickly the clowns, paramedics are at his side. And every other rider is anxiously watching their buddy to see how it will turn out. So Paul spoke to Timothy of sharing his sufferings [II Timothy 1:8]. We're in this together, and only one of us had to nod. But when that commitment was made, it was total. And it always involves others. In I Corinthians 12:26 we read it the best: "And whether one member suffer, all the members suffer with it; or one member be honored, all the members rejoice with it."

It takes a lot of grit to rodeo whether it is High School Rodeo, the Professionals or a select group such as Barrel Racers or Bull Riders. And the wise rider does a lot of preparing. One of my bull riding friends almost drove me crazy as I was trying to talk with him and he kept the conversation going while at the same time he never stopped squeezing a rubber ball in his hands, first one, then the other. He also lifted weights and ran several miles a day. He intended to win. He prepared. We are told to exercise ourselves unto godliness. That means, get into the Bible, get into prayer, get into fellowships with others. You get ready to ride before the ride. It's too late to prepare when the gate flies open. At the end may you be able to say with Paul: "I have fought a good fight, I have finished my course (ride!), I have kept the faith." [II Timothy 4:7]. A good ending that started with a Total Commitment. It just takes a nod of the head.

3 Twice Owned

God lays two claims to an individual's life. The claim that He Created us; and, the claim that He Saved us. Revelation 4:11 makes the first claim clear: "Thou art worthy, O Lord, to receive glory and honor and power: for Thou hast created all things, and for Thy pleasure they are and were created." God is simply stating, "I made you, therefore I own you."

In Revelation 5:9-10 we read: "Thou (Christ) art worthy to take the book (the title deed to the earth), and to open the seals thereof; for Thou wast slain, and hast redeemed us to God by Thy blood out of every kindred and tongue, and people, and nation, and hast made us unto our God kings and priests: and we shall reign on the earth." God bought us by Creation, lost us in sin, and bought us back at Calvary. We are twice owned.

I thought of that in the fall of 2007. Opal and I had gone back to Miracle Mountain Ranch for a few days from our ministry in Wisconsin. While rambling around I saw a used saddle for sale which was not with the regular used tack of the ranch, and it sure did look familiar. The more I studied it over the more sure I became that this was a saddle which once belonged to our daughter, Melodie, some thirty years ago. The story that unfolded made me think of being twice owned.

For twenty years in the beginning of our Ranch ministries, I started all of the colts we raised from our good Quarter Horse stallions and mares, with a few Appaloosas thrown in which we had also raised. There comes a time in the process when someone else must step up on the colt to see if he has really learned and will respond correctly for a different rider. That's where Melodie stepped in. During the earlier years, it was Opal that took the next steps in riding a colt and she has ridden them, been bucked off, rolled on, got back up and ridden a lot of them successfully. Melodie was always "daddy's girl" and it wasn't long before she wanted to be the next rider, so she stepped in line and both girls rode for me. Melodie had a lot of bad rides which she lost and it dawned on me that her saddle, a slick fork, was about the real cause of it all. I began to shop through the catalogs for a new saddle. And, though we could not really afford it, God provided and the day came when the saddle arrived. On a roper tree, hand carved, with a fifteen inch swell. It looked like it was ready to fly.

That winter, after a snow fall of about ten inches, I brought in three other riders and we went out to the back forty where I made an enormous circle and put two lines across it, cutting it into quarters. I had five two year olds that I had started and we were going to put some "learnin" on 'em by playing "Fox and Geese," where the one who is "It" chases someone else till he can tag them and make them it. This would require some reining, trotting, and some loping. Good lessons. Melodie, by this time, had put some hours on her new saddle and had gotten the feel of it. I was clear across this huge circle when I heard her scream. She was being pursued by the "It" and as she kicked her buckskin into a lope, he came unglued. She screamed for she was sure she was going to end up on her head in the snow. By this time all eyes were glued on her and I was pleased to see those lanky legs make contact with those fifteen inch swells and in so doing saw her pick up the rhythm of the horse, then take her seven foot reins and begin to really educate him that it was not nice to buck! And she won.

That saddle was worth every dollar (and there were a lot) I had put in it. She rarely ever bucked off again.

She grew up some more and went to college. To gain finances, she sold her horses and her tack. The saddle was gone. That day in 2007 I was looking at it again. It had been brought to the ranch on assignment to get it sold and had been there a year. I think God had it waiting for me. A few phone calls later the price was determined, the saddle and check passed on the way. I owned the saddle again – and I had paid for it twice. After a few weeks, I took it one night to Cowboy Country Church to see how observant my country people were. They passed the test greatly seeing how I had worked over the saddle.

"You gotta new copper rivet in that near "D" ring." And he was right. "Those are new straps on the breast collar and a new long latigo," yelled out another. Right again. "That sure is a new cinch, or ain't been rode much," was again on target. It was brand new. What I thought no one would notice was finally picked up. "You've taken it apart and oiled it through and through." As I shared the gospel, everyone caught on easily.

God had created us, put us (in Adam and Eve) in the garden of Eden with just one command to keep. Satan lured them into breaking the command by convincing them that God was holding back on them by such restrictions and that they could "be as gods," not needing God at all. Satan told Christ in Luke 4:6 "All this power will I give Thee (Jesus), and the glory of them: for that is delivered unto me; and to whomseover I will I give it." Yes, he gained that when he usurped it from Adam and Eve. Men and women are still trying to be gods without God to this day. But God planned a way back.

He sent Christ to become like us, to die in our place, shedding His blood as payment for our sins. Those who bowed the knee and received Him as Lord and Savior, were bought back by this precious sacrifice and again belonged to God. Peter stated it well: "Ye know that ye were not redeemed with corruptible things, as silver and gold, from your vain conversation received by tradition from your faithers: But with the precious blood of Christ, as of a lamb without blemish and without spot." [I Peter 1:18, 19].

We had so messed up our lives living in sin, that God has had to "replace" some parts in all of us to make us useable once more. And He filled us with His Holy Spirit. "But ye are not in the flesh, but in the Spirit, if so be that the Spirit of God dwell in you. Now if any man have not the Spirit of Christ, he is none of His." [Romans 8:9]. Oil has always been a symbol of the Holy Spirit in the Bible. God saves us, takes us apart, makes all things new and fills us with the Holy Spirit.

That saddle will not be sold again. Nor will God's children be lost again. We've been "twice owned," and are now ready to be used to bring Him glory.

4 The Wages of Sin is Death

That truth comes from Romans 6:23 which, in full, states: "For the wages of sin is death, but the gift of God is eternal life through Christ Jesus our Lord."

My wife has on occasions such as birthdays, Father's Day, anniversaries, etc., been buying me the reprinted books of cowboy author Will James. He was the real thing and wrote twenty-four books in his later years of life with his own illustrations. He was authentic and he was good. Among the good horses of which he wrote, you may have read: "Smokey the Cow-horse," written in 1926. He also wrote of others, the ones that are just born with a resistance to ever being broke. Some are made outlaws by careless and often cruel handling. Those are the horses who will come over on a rider, or, in bucking, come down to the ground without their feet under them, regardless of what it might do to them. They will jump off a hundred foot cliff, run themselves into a wall or tree and break their neck. They do not intend to be ridden, or to submit. They will pay any price for that strange sort of freedom.

In that sixth chapter of Romans, the word "sin" is used seventeen times, and some form of the word death is also used seventeen times. It took me a while to realize that the word "sins" is never used. The point is that "sin" is what we are, and "sins" are what we do. What we do does not make us a sinner, we are that from birth. What we are makes us sin which we do by nature and by choice. John wrote about that and said "If we say that we have no sin, we deceive ourselves, and the truth is not n us." [I John 1:8]. In great contrast, we read that Christ did not have sin in Him. "For He (God) hath made Him (Christ) to be sin for us, Who knew no sin; that we might be made the righteousness of God in Him." [II Corinthians 5:21].

I've only encountered one horse like that in my life, a horse so filled with hatred to man and surrender to man that he would stop at nothing to have his own way. Lew had called me up,while he was on the road for the Lord and told me that there was a horse down in Pittsburg, PA which was being given to the Ranch and would I go get it? Yep, I would and I did. Before Lew hung up he said with great urgency in his voice: "Dad, whatever you do, don't try to ride that horse." Since we have a great relationship I did not ask why, just said I would keep off him. Isn't it fun to always be the first one to ride the "new" horse? After Lew returned home he used that horse several times in "Sermon on the Mount" demonstrations, and every time that horse simply got more wicked. I warned Lew several times to just get rid of him. He kept replying: "Dad, there's one more good sermon illustration in him." The whole thing came to an end suddenly one Saturday as the horse was being used in a demonstration. He was simply being led when for no known reason he suddenly balked, threw himself backward and hit the ground, breaking his neck. The audience gasped and some screamed. Lew calmly yet forcefully quoted Proverbs 29:1 "He, that being often reproved hardeneth his neck, shall suddenly be reproved, and that without remedy." There is an end to it all when least expected. In the sixth chapter of Romans, Paul goes on to make several things clear to the reader.

The only way to deal with sin, what we are, is to take it to the Cross. Our "old man," which ran "the body of sin," is crucified with Christ, that we should no longer be slaves to sin. The life now lived, after

20

the experience at the cross is Christ's life lived through us. A decision is involved there as well. The question is raised: "Know ye not, that to whom ye yield yourselves servants to obey, his servants ye are to whom ye obey; whether of sin unto death, or of obedience unto righteousness?" You were the slaves of sin, but you made a choice from the heart, an obedience from the heart and were set free from the law of sin and death. From that point on you were enabled to be a slave to righteousness.

I like the question that follows such reasoning: "What fruit had ye then in those things whereof ye are now ashamed? For the end of those things is death." [Romans 6:21]. The answer is nothing. And the joy is, that the shame has been forgiven and I am free to live for Christ and bring forth fruit for His glory and for my joy.

Does that mean I will never sin again? No. God has not yet saved our body. This body of ours with its five senses is still very much in tune with this world and its temptations. God does not want us to fall into some aspect of sinning, as John wrote in I John chapter two, but, knowing we were capable of sinning, God made it clear that Christ would be our defense lawyer, pleading our case to God and that if we "confess our sins, He is faithful and just to forgive us our sins, and to cleanse us from all unrighteousness."[I John 1:9]. We have made a choice, and though tempted and tested, we find ourselves to be victors and not victims to sin, to sins, and the wages that they pay.

Paul actually gave the standard when he started the chapter: "What shall we say then? Shall we continue in sin that grace may abound? God forgivd. How sahll we, that are dead to sin, live any longer therein?" [Romans 6:1-2]. You are free to glorify the Lord and live free from the bondage of sin and death. The choice is yours. The means are God's.

5 Form to Function

I had been watching Dale Wilkinson, the only trainer who's been inducted into the American Quarter Horse Association, National Cutting Horse Association and National Reining Horse Association Halls of Fame, train a horse at his ranch and training facility in Waynesboro, Georgia. We then went into his house for a great supper prepared by his wife, Lucy. Afterward, while Lucy and Opal visited, we returned to the barn where Dale showed me one of his yearlings for which he had great hopes in the world of cutting horses. My first impression was a feeling of great surprise to see how small this horse was, as Dale had told me about him before bringing him out of his stall. Though small, he was wonderfully well balanced. He was built to do the job: form to function. I've often wondered how he made out with him.

In Philippians 2:5-8 God describes the coming of Christ with these words: "Let this mind be in you, which was also in Christ Jesus: Who, being in the form of God, thought it not robbery to be equal with God: But made Himself of no reputation, and took upon Him the form of a servant, and was made in the likeness of men: And being found in fashion as a man, He humbled himself and became obedient unto death, even the death of the cross."

I learned through such things that most cutting horses are small. Most race horses are lean and long. Most pulling horses are stout and heavy. They are built to do the job for which they have been selected. This is exactly why Jesus Christ was born of the virgin Mary in a stable (what a great place for a Shepherd to be born!) so long ago. He, God, came to earth, took upon Himself a human form so that He might do as a man what He could not do as God. As a man He could die and become our substitute in the payment of the penalty for sin. And the death He experienced, planned by God and made clear even in Psalm 22 and in Isaiah 53, was the cruel death of the Cross. The stable was not the big thing. The big thing was that God had become a man in order to do what needed to be done to redeem the mankind that God had created and loved.

Throughout the Old Testament we have records of multiplied thousands of cattle, sheep, goats being sacrificed for the sins of mankind, but none of those took away the sin of mankind, that evil which was within the very heart of every person on earth. God made this clear when He had recorded in Hebrews 9:13,14 "For if the blood of bulls and of goats, and the ashes of a heifer, sprinkling the unclean, sanctifieth to the purifying of the flesh (i.e. cleansing us of the sins we had committed): How much more shall the blood of Christ, Who through the eternal Spirit offered Himself without spot to God, purge your conscience from dead works to serve the living God?" Only the blood of Christ cleansed the inside of the individual. He was specifically formed and sent to do that work. Thus, it is recorded of Christ, "Wherefore when he cometh into the world, he saith, 'Sacrifice and offering thou wouldest not, but a body hast thou prepared me: In burnt offerings and sacrifices for sin thou hast had no pleasure.' Then said I, 'Lo, I come (in the volume of the book it is written of me) to do Thy will, O God.'" [Hebrews 10:5-7].

And that will of God governed His life as He had been purposely formed to fulfill that will. He told His disciples that "My meat is to do the will of Him Who sent Me, and to finish His work." [John 4:34].

That was so strong in his mind and heart that even as He faced Calvary and the agony there, He could pray; "Abba, Father, all things are possible unto Thee; take this cup from Me, nevertheless, not what I will, but what Thou wilt." [Mark 14:36].

God made you in the same purposeful way and asks of you the same thing He asked of Christ. In Romans 12:1, God asks us to give our bodies to Him as a living sacrifice which is holy and acceptable to Him. God makes it clear that He gave to those bodies individual gifts by which we are to serve Him. In Romans 12:6-8, the gifts are listed which motivate us to serve Him: prophecy, ministry, teaching, exhortation, giving, leadership, and showing mercy. Gifted for a purpose, form to function, God is asking us to surrender to Him that body, with those gifts, to do His will which is reasonable, good, acceptable and perfect.

As I looked over the beautiful colt that Dale Wilkinson was showing me, I thought ahead to what he could become under the skilled hands of this master horseman. It would take time and constant yielding on the part of the horse for that goal to be achieved. But he was built for it, the raw goods were all there. Just so with your life, you are built for a purpose, provided with the gifts needed. The elements of time and yieldedness under the hands of the Master are as demanding, if not more so, if we are to become all that God has ordained and prepared us to be.

Accepting the fact that God has made us with a purpose, our prayer must be the prayer of our Lord, "Lo, I come to do thy will, O God." [Hebrews 10:7]. It will take daily surrender.

25

6 Swappin' Horses

Probably the greatest horse-trader the world has ever known was King Solomon. When God describes his horse activities we learn that he had 1,400 chariots, 12,000 horsemen and 40,000 stalls for his horses. [II Chronicles 1:13-17; I Kings 4:26].

He had his horses imported from Egypt and Keveh (Cilicia, i.e. Turkey). Then he exported them to all the kings of the Hittites and the kings of Syria. God even gives us the price he got for them: 600 shekels for a chariot and 150 shekels for a horse. Today that would be about $32,000 for the chariot (like a good pick-up truck) and $8,000 for the horse, about the right price for a good horse. With that many horses and those kinds of prices, he must have done a lot of swapping and trading.

Perhaps he had some of that in mind when he penned Proverbs 20:14: "It is naught, it is naught, saith the buyer: but when he is gone his way, then he boasteth." How easy it is to put down the other person's mount, to find those faults of ringbone, spavins, shying and just to let that person know he really isn't offering much of a horse. Then, when you get it at your price, how sweet to brag about getting

27

such a dynamic, trained, competent animal at such a bargain. Things haven't changed much in the swappin' industry.

Getting beat on a horse trade usually does not bring you to the end of life, or the end of your world, but there is a swap of which Christ warned us that has eternal consequences. "And when He had called the people unto Him with His disciples also, He said unto them, 'Whoseover will come after Me, let him deny himself, and take up his cross, and follow Me. For whosoever will save his life shall lose it; but whoseover shall lose his life for My sake and the Gospel's, the same shall save it. For what shall it profit a man if he shall gain the whole world and lose his own soul? Or what shall a man give in exchange for his soul?'" [Mark 8:34-37]. Putting it bluntly, Christ is asking, "How will you swap for your soul?"

Somehow Solomon did not follow his own advice and we discover in the Word of God that he swapped his relationship with God for the love of women. God had warned him from the beginning of the kingship that he should not amass horses, money or women. He did all three, but that which turned his heart away from God was the women. I have often wondered if he will be in heaven. It seems he will be, trusting that the book of Ecclesiastes was written from his heart when he wrote of all of the vanities of life, then concluded that men ought to "Fear God and keep His commandments, for this is the whole duty of man. For God shall bring every work into judgment, with every secret thing, whether it be good or whether it be evil." [Ecclesiastes 12:13,14]. But he made a poor swap.

Eve made her swap earlier and it cost her dearly. She swapped a piece of fruit for peace of mind (fear came in) and the loss of her home and freedom from pain in childbirth. We talk of the "Now" generation as though it was a new thing with its desire for instant gratification. The "Now" generation was active "then" in the garden of Eden. She fell for the line that God did not love her and Adam and was holding back on them.

King Saul traded the sparing of a life, King Agag whom God told him to destroy, for his kingdom and for the peace which he once had with

God. He lived in fear for the rest of his life, continually went down hill spiritually, and lost his life in battle because he had turned his back on God.

Demas traded ministry with Paul, the greatest missionary-evangelist the world has known, for a fling at the world. I've often wondered how his life and adventure turned out. Christ gave us the question, He never gave us all of the answers.

Did you ever wonder what Judas Iscariot was planning on doing with what he had stolen as the treasurer of the disciples; and, what would now have been made possible with the additional thirty pieces of silver he had gained when he swapped the betrayal of Christ for the money? This was one swap so terrible that God had a special place of torment to which Judas went. [Acts 1:25].

People continue to make such swaps in life. How often we read and hear of athletes, politicians, celebrities, and, sadly, pastors and other men of God, who have made swaps and trades from which they thought they would benefit, only to discover that they were the losers. Some losing for eternity.

There is no way of knowing how to compare "the whole world," with "lose his own soul." What we do know is that such swaps are made, and the swaps last for eternity. Christ placed His value on a soul when He died in that one's place on Calvary. Where do you place your value? The devil will do his best to get you to swap your soul, but remember, he usually will also want a little to boot in the deal.

7 Free Indeed

Having watched a couple of Roy Roger movies and seeing the marvelous abilities of Trigger, I was really intrigued by an article in the July 2008, Western Horseman magazine. On page 133 it was stated that Glenn Randall, Jr. had taught Trigger "to respond to more than 30 visual, and 58 verbal commands." On the screen Trigger always looked so free, so knowing, yet it was only an illusion. He was always obeying a command from his trainer. I even thought then of the "Liberty Horses" I had watched in a circus or two. Again, their liberty was only an illusion as they were completely controlled by their trainer, though distanced from him or her.

Freedom! A word which describes what everyone longs for and struggles to achieve. Sometimes the word excites us as we think of someone or something that is FREE! We that work with horses are led to believe that mustangs are free, but I have reason to question even that.

There were, according to a Bureau of Land Management web site (June, 2008), 35,000 horses and 7,000 burros in 1998, living in ten Western States. These are described as "unbranded, unclaimed, free roaming horse or burro found on BLM or U.S. Forest Service administered land in the western United States." They are "protected by the Wild Free Roaming Horse and Burro Act of 1971." Perhaps the word "controlled" could be substituted for the word "protected" in the sentence. I find that the freedom comes at a price to us the taxpayers. To "protect" these "free roaming" animals costs the United States $50,000 per week, amounting to some 16 million dollars a year. Freedom may be only illusionary; and, it always comes at a price which someone must pay.

That's how real freedom came to us. In John 8:32, we read: "And you shall know the truth, and the truth shall make you free." Free from the bondage to fear and the bondage to sin which always result from believing the lies of the enemy, Satan. From here on out everything in life is to be tested by the searchlight of the Holy Word of God. That which is not of the Scriptures, or contrary to the Scriptures is a lie to be discarded. There is a greater emphasis in John 8:36 stating: "Therefore if the Son makes you free, you shall be free indeed." This is God's Promise of Freedom. Some argued with Christ that they had never been in bondage to anyone. In verse 34, Christ gave the proof of that bondage when He stated: "whosoever committeth sin is the servant of sin." Since all have sinned, all are classified as slaves to sin. The only One who can liberate an individual from sin is the Person of Jesus Christ. There is a hymn which states it well: "And when before the throne, I stand in Him complete, 'Jesus died my soul to save,' my lips shall still repeat. Jesus paid it all, all to Him I owe; sin had left a crimson stain, He washed it white as snow."

The place where it all began, this freedom in Christ, was at the cross. In Galatians 2:20 a marvelous exchange is declared: "I am crucified with Christ: nevertheless I live; yet not I, but Christ liveth in me: and the life which I now live in the flesh I live by the faith of the Son of God, who loved me, and gave Himself for me." The Bible repeatedly declares that it is all by grace, not by works, not by the law.

The "I" life, actually controlled by Satan, which held me in bondage to sin while allowing me to think I was free, having life MY way, was destroyed at the Cross and the new life is one directed by the indwelling Holy Spirit whom God has given to me to enable me to glorify Christ and to be free from the control of sin in this new walk in life.

In this new-found freedom, there is a practice which God requires of us to maintain this life of freedom in Christ. In Galatians 5:24, God reveals that "And they that are Christ's have crucified the flesh with the affections and lusts." God, by His Holy Spirit, had brought me to the Cross where I was crucified with Christ by that outside working. Now, God tells me that it is my responsibility to take the flesh, better understood as the five unconverted senses we each have (touch, taste, smell, sight, and hearing) and bring those to the cross that I might continue to live in freedom from the bondage of sin into which this flesh would bring me. This problem is why Christ told us in Luke 9:23 that we are to take up our cross daily as we follow Him.

This "flesh" holds within itself both evil desires and good desires. We are responsible, through Christ, to take those desires to the Cross, whether good or bad, that would hinder us in living out the will of God in our lives. Freed from the bondage of sin and the bondage to sin, we are, thereby, free indeed.

8 Running Back to the Source

I was privileged to be riding with Warren Davis, cowboss of the CS Ranch in Cimarron, New Mexico, his wife, Mary, and other cowhands, gathering cattle to be weaned and branded. We had moved them about four miles and had about all of them inside a trap where they would be held until the next morning. Suddenly I heard Warren call out: "Get those calves." Three of them had been dragging behind the herd and now missed the gate where their mothers were. Instead, they had turned abruptly and began running back to where we had gathered them. Two other cowboys and myself spun our horses around and each headed out for one of the calves. The other two roped their calves quite handily and my horse had scored well on the calf I was following. Then it dawned on me, I did not have a catch rope! We were moving along in a nice even lope with my horse right behind the calf, and I thought of step number two. Getting into rhythm with the horse as he ran, I just stepped off of him, ran about six giant steps, grabbed the calf and flanked him to the ground. Problem number two, I also did not have a pigging string! No problem!

I just pulled the thin belt off of my chaps and tied the calf up with the belt. Third problem: the calf kicked that nicely tied belt into three pieces! My rescue came from a Mexican lad, son of one of the cowboys, riding his motor scooter. He saw my predicament, and we had a good laugh together. Then he returned to his scooter where he happened to have a piece of rubber coated wire with which we tied up the calf once more, and waited for the pickup truck to come along where he could be taken back to the trap and find his mother.

When I got back to the trap, I was asked why I had gotten off my horse, so had to explain the whole situation for the enjoyment of the crew. Then, being ignorant, I asked, "Why were you so anxious for us to get those calves?" The answer was simple. When a cow and calf are separated they always return to the place where the calf last nursed and there await the return of the other. Will James, noted cowboy author and artist, who had worked on the CS in the early 1920's made the same observation in a couple of the stories he wrote. They always return to the source. And had we not caught them as we did, we would have had a long afternoon filled with a long ride and a troublesome time to catch them.

Back at the source, with the mother cow, all fear would be gone under her protecting shadow. Every want would be supplied as the nursing process took place. And rest, especially after the miles of being driven, would be found laying down in her shadow. Like that calf, we all wrestle with fear, needs to be supplied, and rest. There is a source of supply for the believer, and that Source is Jesus Christ. In the Scriptures I find seven reasons to run back often to Him, my source of supply.

1. When hungering and longing, I recall His statement in John 6:32-35, "I AM the Bread of life." Not only that, He is the Living Bread of Life. The supply is not only satisfying, but absolutely inexhaustible.

2. Sometimes my problem is that I don't know which way to turn, or, am afraid in the "dark" periods of life where everything is uncertain. It is then that I hear Him say from John 8:12, "I AM the Light

of the world." No matter how dark it is, I get my focus and direction by looking to Him, not looking at the circumstances or just wandering about in the dark.

3. At times I become weary in life and in the tasks before me and need refreshed before I can go on. In John 10:7,9, Christ makes it clear: "I AM the door." And, if we enter into the sheepfold through Him we find protection and rest. He also states that we are free to "go in and out and find pasture." Everything I need in my exhaustion and concerns, is found in Christ. Truly, my strength and hope is renewed.

4. Everyone is born with a need to be loved, and to give forth love. There are times in life when one doubts if ANYONE loves him at all. There is an absolute emotional emptiness that can make one wonder if life is worth the living. It is then I run back to the Source and He tells me. "I AM the good Shepherd." [John 10:11,14]. The One Who loved me enough to die for me, Who seeks me on the mountains of my lostness and aloneness and emptiness. The hireling, He states does not love me like that. He himself flees when the danger comes. The Good Shepherd will face the danger for me, even at the cost of His life.

5. How often times I stand at the casket of a friend and ponder life and death. How often, unsolicited, the fear of death comes to the individual. Fear is a terrible emotion, referred to over 400 times in the Bible. He speaks to me as He did to Martha and Mary, saying, "I AM the resurrection and the life." [John 11:25]. I'll be with you in death, even as I have been with you in life. In fact, at the tomb of Lazarus is where the brief verse is given: "Jesus wept." [John 11:35]. Don't be afraid, run back to the Source. He is there, and He loves you and weeps with you.

6. From teenage and all through life, the questions arise as to what we are to do, to be, where we are to live, to work, who we are to marry, and the list goes on. At the Source, the words are almost shouted: "I AM the Way, the Truth, and the Life." [John 14:6]. He had said earlier, "Follow Me." Just don't stop. He still is the Answer

to the question: "What's next?"

7. We all like to feel productive, to feel that we have made some mark in life, contributed something, that is worthwhile. In John 15:1,5, Christ states that: "I AM the Vine." As we abide in Him and He and His word abides in us, we will bring forth fruit...more fruit... much fruit. The relationship is the answer.

God makes it as clear to His child as the cow and calf understand each other, every need is met by running back to the Source.

9 Motivation

Got me a new horse, a pretty one. He is bright sorrel, blaze face, three white stockings and one white sock. Made me think of a little ditty I learned from a Simco saddle dealer from whom I bought saddles for our youth ranch. It referred to horses with chrome: "One white foot, buy him; two white feet, shy him; three white feet, deny him; four white feet and a strip on the nose, knock him in the head and feed him to the crows." I wasn't about to do that. The thought that entered my mind was: With a horse as pretty as this, if I could teach him some tricks I could use him to preach the Gospel of Jesus Christ. I had done that in the past and this looked like a good prospect for the future. As I thought of that, God took me a step further and brought a truth to my mind that challenged and humbled me.

My basis for teaching, training is familiar to all: Make the right thing easy and the wrong thing hard. This is a gentle, successful way in the field of training. Today some trainers use "clickers" in the training process and have good success. Whatever is used, the key is "reward!" And, that is perfectly Scriptural even for spiritual growth as well as training anything.

The writer of the book of Hebrews stated: "But without faith it is impossible to please Him (God): for he that cometh to God must believe that He is, and that He is a rewarder of them that diligently seek Him." [Hebrews 11:6]. The steps are simple: Belief in the existence of God – or the trainer; expectation of a reward for right performance; and, a need to be focused, "diligently seek Him." When those three things line up, learning occurs. The idea, of course, is to get to the place where the act is performed because of the relationship of the trainer and horse, of God and His child, not just because of the reward. I see this developed in the life of Christ and His followers.

Not long into the reading of the book of John you will find Christ facing His followers with this accusation: "Jesus answered them and said, 'Verily, verily, I say unto you, ye seek Me, not because ye saw the miracles, but because ye did eat of the loaves, and were filled.'" [John 6:26]. They had long turned from the fellowship and following of Christ to where their only thought was the table and more bread. My new horse about did the same thing. My eyes saw quite quickly that the first thing he really learned was where I kept the goodies on my person with which he was rewarded. His nose ALWAYS went there first. I had a notion to change his name to "Mooch." How easy it is to develop a "welfare case mentality," in our relationship with Christ. He does not want that. How easy then to turn our backs on Him when He is not providing the fun and games and refreshments we have come to believe are our rights in Christ. Somehow the Cross is exchanged for the Cuisine. And the reward is the exalted thing, not the Rewarder. The grossness of sin, recorded in Romans 1 can be explained by verse 21 "Because that, when they knew God, they glorified Him not as God, neither were thankful; but became vain in their imaginations, and their foolish heart was darkened."

The actions of obedience and performance because of the rewards must come to a new cause. Christ makes that cause very clear. In one of His resurrection appearances to seven disciples on a fishing trip, Christ singled out Peter and faced him with the issue of his love. "Do you love me more than these?" was the question posed three times. Perhaps because Peter had denied Him three times. There were also three other things present which may have been meant. All were Peter's because of God's grace. Perhaps a sort of reward. I can hear Christ ask: "Peter do you love Me more than you love the men I have given you as companions and friends?" "Peter, do you love me more than the boat I have allowed you to own, and have graced by my using it for a pulpit on occasion?" "Peter, do you love Me more than the great load of fish I gave, which you could hardly drag to shore?" Things. Rewards. And all we have has come from God because of His great love for us. There is nothing wrong with loving those persons and things which Christ has bestowed upon us. The issue is, do we love Christ more? This is the real motivation for service, for doing what our Lord wants us to do. Peter had heard this before.

In John 14:15 the word is clear, "If ye love Me, keep My commandments." And verse 21 "He that hath My commandments and keepeth them, it is he that loveth Me: and he that loveth Me shall be loved by My Father, and I will love him and manifest Myself to him." John wrote of this again in a later year and put it clearly: "For this is the love of God, that we keep His commandments: and His commandments are not grievous." [I John 5:3]. Because of our love for Him Who loved us unto His death on the cruel cross, we serve Him. Not for reward, not for personal benefit, just because we love Him and have had it made clear to us that THIS is His will for our lives. It is a change of motivation that He demands.

10 Whatever it Takes, God Provides

Having been intrigued by the life of Saul who became Paul, from his conversion to Christ in Acts 9, I was rather surprised to get to Acts 23 and find Paul riding a horse! Throughout his ministries he is constantly seen walking or going by boat to reach a destination. But a horse? The story behind that and the provision of God is fascinating and comforting.

The episode starts out with Paul's unnamed nephew overhearing a plot by over forty men to kill Paul as he is being brought on a journey, supposedly as part of his trial. He hurries to the prison, informs a guard who takes him to Paul, then to the commander and Paul's life is spared by one of God's strange provisions.

Sometimes on life's trail it is good to backtrack and pick up additional information. One of God's repeated truths in that somebody always knows what is going on. Just as Paul's nephew knew of the plot, there are many cases where God makes it clear that somebody knows and that knowledge is vital.

For example: Boaz and all of the people of his village knew that Ruth was a virtuous woman. [Ruth 2:3; 3:11]. When King Ahasuerus wanted to execute wicked Haman, Harbonah, a eunuch, knew that Haman had a gallows in his back yard on which he intended to hang Mordecai. [Esther 7:9]. When the two spies sent by Joshua got to Jericho, the king knew they were there, and that they were in Rahab's house. [Joshua 2:2]. I found at least 32 incidents recorded in God's word where somebody knew what was going on and it was a vital knowledge in the lives of others.

Above all, God always knows. "He that planted the ear, shall He not hear? He that formed the eye, shall He not see? [Psalm 94:9]. "Neither is there any creature that is not manifest in His sight: but all things are naked and opened unto the eyes of Him with whom we have to do." [Hebrews 4:13].

A second truth that God makes clear on the trail of life, is that He has no "Lone Rangers" in his service. That boy, that nephew, was needed in the life of Paul. Christ sent the twelve out two by two. Later He sent seventy disciples out to proclaim the Gospel. They too went out two by two. When the body of an individual is used to illustrate the Body of Christ in I Corinthians 12, the picture is eye to hand, head to feet, if one member suffers, all do. If one is honored, all rejoice. The church is not suffering today, as some think, because a few are "running it." The problem is not those few, but rather the many who are not using the gifts God gave them for the edifying of the body, doing nothing for Christ. Even in the incident before us there were two centurions, two hundred soldiers, seventy horsemen and two hundred spearmen. There is a place for you in the service of the King.

I was humbled, since I think so highly of horses, to realize that God did not put a lot of stock in the horse, but He did use it in this case. Of horses, David wrote: "Some trust in chariots, some in horses, but we will remember the name of the Lord our God." [Psalm 20:7]. Or, in Psalm 33:17, "A horse is a vain thing for safety." (Though God did use one in Paul's life). Psalm 147:10, "He (God) delighteth not in the strength of the horse." The real truth is, whatever it takes, God provides. "And the Lord shall deliver me from every evil work." [II Timothy 4:18]. By whatever means it takes. Don't put God in a box which would limit Him.

And God gave Paul the ability to ride the horse on a tremendous journey. Remember, he was a tentmaker, not an equestrian. He walked, he rode boats. At 9:00 P.M., the third hour of the night, with the great military accompaniment, Paul left for Antipatris, a journey of 40 miles. From there, continuing with the calvary unit, he rode on to Caesarea, another 25 miles. 65 miles, and, evidently, in one night. That would be quite a ride for anyone, let alone a tentmaker. Perhaps Paul was quoting to himself what he wrote later to the church at Philippi. "I can do all things through Christ which strengthens me." {Philippians 4:13]. And he made it.

You are unique in your present situation. You are not alone in it. God knows all about it, and others of whom you would not dream know. One of the great delights in life is to meet the scores of people who surprise you by stating that they pray for you consistently, and have for years without your knowing it.

Furthermore, God will provide for you in this unexpected period of your life. You are not hidden from His sight. Nothing is too big, too hard, too impossible for God. Whatever it takes, God provides. He may even let you ride a horse!

11 Being Able to Read

I was following a car which had this bumper sticker: "If you can read this, thank a Teacher." Good thought. The importance of reading came to me strongly as I was doing an internship at the Moccasin Bend Hospital in Chattanooga, Tennessee. I was working in the alcohol and drug ward. Beside me sat a delightful, friendly man, bound by alcoholism and longing to be "out" for a weekend. To gain this privilege, he had to pass a certain test. I sat beside him to not only read him the questions, but then to write down his answers. I had to write his answers? Yes, he gave them to me verbally, but he could not read nor write. And he was good, he knew the right answers. Then in quiet words, he shared with me that this inability was one of the strong factors, that in depression over his being so limited, had driven him to drink. He had never been able to get ahead in life, to become what he wanted to be because he could not read.

In years past, many men and women had no, or limited, educations. For many in the cowboy world the inability to read was a common factor. Yet these were not ignorant men. Many were brilliant in ways beyond those who could formally read. They knew multitudes of brands on cattle and horses plus multitudes of ear markings on the cattle. They could track a herd of livestock or a single horse. They knew as well, it seems, or better, how to forecast the weather than some of the reports we get from sophisticated sources today. They, with the "uneducated" Indians of our land, could read almost invisible "signs" along a trail. They could read, but their "books" were not the ordinary ones of life. Will Rogers, the great cowboy philosopher put it in these words: "All of us are ignorant, only on different subjects."

God expects us to read. We are to "search the Scriptures," to "study to show ourselves as approved workmen to God." He promises a blessing in one of the most difficult books in the New Testament, the book of Revelation. There in chapter one, verse 3 He inspired John to write: "Blessed is he that readeth, and they that hear the words of this prophecy, and keep those things which are written therein: for the time is at hand." Read, hear, keep - a simple prescription for being blessed. God speaks to hearts as eyes scan His writings.

Revelation 2:4, "Thou hast left thy first love." Is that God's word to you today? How's your love-life with Jesus? He had written for us to read: "If ye love Me, keep My commandments." [John 14:15]. How do you measure up? If you are not where you belong, Christ's word to you is: "Repent."

Revelation 2:10 "Be thou faithful unto death." Most folks are faithful until the blessings from God aren't as plentiful, or until the going gets rough. What has come into your life that makes you doubt God's love to you and makes you believe that it's time to quit? It's always too soon to quit.

Revelation 2:13. God lets us know that these folks lived where Satan lived. The choice was, evidently, not theirs. This was a place of gross immorality. That was a choice they could make. We may be in the world, but the world does not have to be in us. Clean up your act. Romans 6:1,2 make it very clear, as you read it, that sin does not have dominion over us and we do not need to live in it. The issue is: to whom are you yielded, to sin or to righteousness?

Revelation 2:19, "I know thy works, and charity, and service, and faith, and thy patience, and thy works; and the last to be more than the first." And you thought no one noticed. God does. Others do too, though they don't often say, "thanks." Just keep going. Christ had a few things against this Church in Thyatira, but what He mentioned first, for them to read, was that He understood all they were doing for Him. Now it was time to get a bit more done, but you're doing a good job.

Revelation 3:2, "Be watchful." Never are we to let our guard down. God knew here as He knew in 2:19 all about the works, but there was a weakness showing which was leading to death of the ministry. "Remember therefore how you have received and heard, hold fast and repent..." We all stand in the need of revival from time to time. This is enemy territory and we can't afford to fall asleep.

Revelation 3:8. "I have set before thee an open door, and no man can shut it." When God calls to ministry, get going. You may feel financially unable, mentally incompetent, inadequate for the task. Did Christ open the door? Has He spoken to your heart? The desire of God, recorded in I Corinthians chapter one is to take the weak and the unwise and get His job done so that He can gain the glory. You are just what He is looking for.

Revelation 3:15. Lukewarm. "You are neither cold nor hot." There were springs in Laodicea that led to this analogy in the lives of individuals. God can use the hot springs as well as the cold springs. We are not alike. God intended the differences because of the tasks set before us. These folks had a false impression of their having achieved. They really were naked and blind and defiled. "Be zealous therefore and repent." No, it is NOT too late! Remember, we were to be faithful unto death. You aren't dead yet. Therefore there is hope and ministry and blessing. "He who hath an ear, let him hear what the Spirit saith unto the churches." [Revelation 3:22]. The Spirit is still speaking by the Word which He inspired. Read about it.

12 "Look Well"

Those are the words we heard the foreman's wife yell as Opal and I crossed the Cimarron River in New Mexico, in the area of the old Maxwell Land Grant, to make a gathering of cattle. We had been instructed to ride each arroyo, watch every gully and cross every hill. From past years with our own small herd of cattle, we had learned how well a calf can curl up and hide itself so that your horse almost steps on it before it is seen. Sometimes I believe they can hide behind a blade of grass! And they sure won't get up and run until they absolutely have to. The cows are artists too at blending into the backgrounds of trees and rocks. Her advice was good, "Look well."

Evidently we did all right, for when the three sets of riders brought their gatherings together a few hours later the head count was just what was expected. Nothing had been missed. Just so in the reading of the Bible, we need to "look well." It is not enough to just read, as we considered earlier, we need to really study as we are told in II Timothy 2:15. That will take some effort. In John 5:39, Christ told us to search the Scriptures, for "they are they which testify of Me." That is, in those Scriptures He was clearly revealed. And the Scriptures

51

He meant were the writings of the Old Testament. It would be some years after His death and resurrection before the New Testament, in writing, would be started. For a simple, yet rewarding exercise, look for Christ in the Psalms. And, of course, look well! And in your looking, don't neglect the Old Testament. It is the foundation for all we have in the New Testament. Here are a few jewels about Christ in the Psalms.

Christ at Calvary, Psalm 22. Verse one starts out "My God, my God, why hast Thou forsaken Me? Why art Thou so far from helping Me, and from the words of My roaring?" The words are later said in Mark 15:34. Here, centuries earlier, the experience of the cross is vividly seen in verse after verse of the Psalm. In Psalm 69:21, you read of the vinegar offered to Him. Calvary is clearly taught.

Christ our companion, the Shepherd of Psalm 23. Always with us. This will become His promise in Matthew 28:19,20 where it is clearly stated that He will be with us through the end of the world. Note also in Psalm 23 that the sheep is talking ABOUT his Shepherd as the Psalm opens, but when he gets to the valley of the shadow of death, the sheep stops talking ABOUT his Shepherd, and begins to talk TO the Shepherd. Just so in our lives, the valleys of shadows which we all must walk, are intended to drive us into a closer, more personal relationship with the Shepherd.

Christ as crowned is the theme of Psalm 24. He is the "Who is this King of glory? The Lord strong and mighty, the Lord mighty in battle." [Verse 8.]. You will read in I Corinthians 15:25, that "He must reign," and He will. In Revelation 15:3. He is "King of the saints." In 19:16, Christ is "King of kings and Lord of lords." When all of the dust of earth is settled and every mouth of the agnostic, skeptic and atheist is stilled, Christ will be on the throne. "Who is this King of glory? The Lord of hosts, He is the King of glory." [Verse 10].

Christ is coming, Psalm 96. The Psalm starts with the salvation of the Lord in verse 2 and ends with the dynamic words that He is coming to judge the earth, the world with righteousness and the people with His truth. [Verse 13]. In Psalm 98:9, that same truth of His coming is repeated. That truth is so important that in the book of I Thessalonians, the only book in the Bible devoted entirely to the teaching of Christ's coming, emphasized in each of its five chapters, a command is given. I Thessalonians 5:27, "I charge you by the Lord that this epistle be read to all the holy brethren." That command is not found in any other book. That command is the most vital truth for every believer to understand. Christ is coming.

Christ, His character, Psalm 99. In verses 3, 5, and 9, we are clearly taught that He is Holy. Of all people, it is Peter who picks up on this in the New Testament. In I Peter 1:15 we read: "But as He which hath called you is holy, so be ye holy in all manner of conversation." Throughout the Bible you will read: "Holy, Holy, Holy," the cry of the ages describing the very character of God the Father: HOLY; God the Son: HOLY; and, God the Spirit: HOLY. So God expects that of His children as well.

Christ, and the conspirator, Judas Iscariot, Psalm 109. This identification will be made very clear by Peter as he teaches, and quotes from this Psalm in Acts 1:16-20. You would do well to take and read all of Psalm 109 because Peter only deals with that portion wherein the office of Judas is to be given to another. The Psalm, however, goes into great depth to show the full price Judas Iscariot paid for conspiring to betray and sell the Lord Jesus Christ.

Christ, conqueror. Psalm 110:1, "The Lord said to my Lord, 'Sit thou at My right hand, until I make thine enemies thy footstool.'" You who are suffering for Christ, keep one thing in mind, we are on the winning side. Sometimes in a war, a few battles seem lost, but who wins is what counts. Matthew will write this verse in Matthew 22:44, as Jesus quoted it of Himself. And He ties it to David, for it was David who wrote Psalm 110.

Christ, the cornerstone. This is seen so clearly in Psalm 118:22,23. The capstone, the stone which the builders rejected. When that day of victory comes and Christ is the cornerstone of all, we will join in the phrase of the Psalmist who further wrote: "This is the day which the Lord hath made; we will rejoice and be glad in it." [Verse 24].

Peter will quote this, by the Holy Spirit, in I Peter 2:6-8. And we shall "live" to see it. Christ is found throughout the entire Old Testament. But it is imperative that as we read, we "look well."

13 Men Wanted

During the Second World War, the Marines had a recruitment slogan: "The Marines are looking for a few good men." And that appealed to many who became marines and warriors for our country. Men were being looked for in early 1860s as well - for a far different cause.

The request was for men, young, under eighteen, slight of build, under 135 pounds, preferably orphans, and men willing to face death. These were the requirements of those who rode for The Pony Express.

Gentlemen Russels, Majors, and Waddell believed they could make a profit in getting mail across the Western States quicker than was being done. The Pony Express was their dream. The plan was to carry mail 2,000 miles and do it in ten days. It lasted but a short time from April 3, 1860 to October 26, 1861. In the venture which only lasted eighteen months, the three gentlemen lost $200,000.

"Faster, still faster," was their motto with the fastest time from St. Joseph, Missouri to Sacramento, California being made in seven days and seventeen hours. The riders changed horses about every ten miles – if the change stations had not been attacked by Indians or renegades and the replacements stolen.

God was looking for a man in Ezekiel 22. Of Israel He stated: Her priests have violated My law and profaned My holy thing. Her princes are like wolves. Her prophets are like tempered mortar and see false visions. Her people have used oppressions, committed robbery, and mistreated the poor and needy. Possibly some of the saddest words in the Bible describe God's search. [Verse 30]. "And I sought for a man among them, that should make up the hedge, and stand in the gap before me for the land, that I should not destroy it: but I found none." What a tragedy, not one man found to do a work for God.

In the New Testament, in the very formative years of the Church, a search for men to serve God is again instituted. That need and search is revealed in Acts chapter six. There was a need to care for the widows in the church. The apostles were tied up with prayer and the teaching of the Word of God. Were men available for the task? Praise God, the answer was "yes." Seven were needed.

They had to be of good reputation. [Verse 3]. I think of this in light of men God sought to direct the early church as Elders and Deacons in I Timothy 3. They had to be of good report of "those who are without." That is, how did the unsaved view them? It is easy for members of the church to see men with a "good old boy" syndrome in their viewing. How does the world, the unsaved see them? That would be a strong test to be applied today. They also had to be full of the Holy Spirit.

When I think of Christ telling us: "Wherefore by their fruits ye shall know them." [Matthew 7:20]. I like to test a person as to being "full of the Holy Spirit," by Galatians 5:22,23. Where is the love, joy, peace, longsuffering, kindness, goodness, faithfulness, gentleness, self-control in their life? If we are to know men by their fruits, then this fruit of the Spirit must be the final test of a man truly filled by the Holy Spirit.

Being full of wisdom was also a requirement. Wisdom can come in answer to prayer, as James tells us. Wisdom also has two companions: knowledge – get the facts; and understanding – realize what the facts are saying. Those two things are the basis for wisdom. Some men will never be wise because they will not read and search for the facts.

Full of faith was a further requirement, in v. 5. Actually, you can have all of the faith you want. There are three sources of faith. First, it comes by the Word of God, "Faith cometh by hearing and hearing by the Word of God." [Romans 10:17]. Also, it is listed in the "fruit of the Spirit" [Galatians 5:22,23], and, finally, it is a gift from God: "For by grace are ye saved through faith, and that (the faith) not of yourselves, it is the gift of God." [Ephesians 2:8]. Help yourself, it is yours for the taking.

And these men were "full of power." Again, by the Spirit. And by the word, which is the "power of God unto salvation." [Romans 1:16].

As I read all of that, one thing struck me with great conviction. Not just that they took the responsibility, but that they were already ready to take it. These men were not chosen and then trained to become competent. They were men who were already honest, of good reputation, full of the Holy Spirit and wisdom and faith and power. The question that came to my mind was, that if I were to be in a lineup of men to be chosen, would I be ready? Today?

"I will study and prepare, and if my opportunity comes, I will be ready." -Abraham Lincoln.

Would you be?

14 Rejected

The clanging, banging sound as one gate crashed into another was about the only sound heard beyond the bawling of the cattle on a cool morning. We had brought John's cattle in to be pregnancy tested. The very few that were not with calf were turned into another pen by the clever use of two gates. Just by releasing the one, the cow "escaped" into the desired pen, then the gate was closed back up again waiting for the next switch. The released gate would swing across the alley and hit the gate of the next pen. It was noisy, but it was an effective way to sort the cows. I was holding cattle in an alleyway, Gary was cutting out cattle to push them to the chutes and the inspection of the veterinarian. I could not see what was going on, I just heard, but I knew. The word "rejected" came to mind as I heard the gates crash from time to time.

Rejected! What a horrible word. For those cattle it meant a quick trip to the market and from there to a slaughter house. Sure enough, within minutes after the last cow had been checked, a stock trailer was backing into the loading chute and in fifteen minutes the rejected cows were loaded and on the road. They, of course, had no idea of what it meant to be rejected, nor of their future. As I sat on my horse watching the procedure, my mind turned to thoughts from the Scriptures.

The cattle had been rejected because they were not going to produce. There was no "new life" within them. From all outward appearances, one could not really tell that at this time, but a careful checking made it clear. Christ taught us of this on an early morning walk to Jerusalem. He had spent the night in Bethany and was now returning to Jerusalem to continue His teaching ministry. No breakfast had been provided. I've often wondered why not, but it wasn't, and he was hungry. Seeing a fig tree in the distance with leaves on it, he approached it, seeking to find figs for breakfast. He found nothing. The Scriptures make it clear that it was not the time of figs, so why would He have expected to find figs? From the standpoint of production, when the fig tree has leaves, the figs have been formed as well. Though this was not the time for the full crop of figs, there are always, in every crop, "first-ripe" fruits. In the Word of God, we are taught that the first ripe fruits belong to God. [Exodus 22:29]. Thus, Christ, being God, had the right to the first-ripe figs this tree was supposedly bearing. Christ cursed the tree and the next morning the disciples were surprised to see how quickly the tree had dried up. Rejected! [Mark 11:12-14; 20,21].

In Matthew 7:16, 20, Christ made it clear that His followers would be known by their fruits, by what they produced. Because we have His life within us, we are not to be barren. There are at least six kinds of fruits we can bear.

The Fruit of Souls won to Christ. [Proverbs 11:30; John 4:35,36].

The Fruit of the Spirit. [Galatians 5:22,23].

The Fruit of our Substance, our finances. [Philippians 4:16,17; Romans 15:26-28].

The Fruit of our Service. [Colossians 1:10].

The Fruit from our Spankings. Yes, God chastens so that we might bear fruit. [Hebrews 12:11].

The Fruit of our Speech. [Hebrews 13:15].

At times when a believer confronts a brother who has sin in his life, the response is: "Who are you to judge?" The answer is simply: "I'm not here as your judge, I'm speaking as a fruit inspector." Christ had gone on to say that those whom He rejected as He inspected their fruit were "workers of iniquity." Those who do not produce are culled.

We need to heed the words of Peter: "Wherefore the rather, brethren, give diligence to make your calling and election sure: for if ye do these thigns, ye shall never fall." [II Peter 1:10]. Don't play games with salvation. You are dealing with eternal values.

Paul put it in these words in I Corinthians 9:27. "But I keep under my body, and bring it into subjection: lest that by any means, when I have preached to others, I myself should be a castaway." Neither Peter nor Paul took their redemption in Christ and their service for Him as a light thing.

God expects a change in the life of a person professing faith in Christ. There is a new life indwelling, and God expects that individual to produce for His glory. Romans 6:20-22 spells it out clearly: "For when ye were the servants of sin, ye were free from righteousness. What fruit had ye then in those things whereof ye are now ashamed? For the end of those things is death. But now being made free from sin, and become servants to God, ye have your fruit unto holiness, and the end everlasting life."

God expects us to produce!

15 Your Speech Betrays You

Peter tried hard to be near Christ at His trial and yet to remain "invisible" so that the crowd would not recognize him as a follower of the Lord. He had two problems that were faced. First, he looked like one of those who followed Christ. Then, he talked like one from the area where Christ lived and labored. Matthew recorded it: "Surely thou also art one of them; for thy speech betrayeth thee." [Matthew 26:73]. Mark penned it: "Surely thou art one of them: for thou art a Galilaean, and thy speech agreeth thereto." [Mark 14:70]. His denial led to his cursing, followed by bitter conviction as Christ turned and looked at him. His speech had truly betrayed him.

In the world of the livestock industry, particularly the world of horses and cattle, we find ourselves indebted to and identified with those who speak the Spanish language. Or, as it is called by some, Mexican, or even Tex-Mex. But it is an identifiable language and it marks those who use it.

Sombrero for hat. Chaps, chinks, chaparajos (to protect from the thorny chaparral bush). Riata, a rope of leather. Maguay, rope from the fibers of the century plant. Vaquero, buckaroo, a cowperson.

Cavvy, a herd of horses. Savvy, from sabe, he knows. Hackamore, jaquima, a halter. Bueno, lobo, zorro, amigo, and rodeo, from rodear, to surround, to encircle. And, we like to part with A Dios! With God. The list is not endless, but it is long. We owe so much to our Mexican friends and their language.

God is interested in your speech and fills the Scriptures with admonitions concerning it. James writes that the tongue is an untamed evil. In Colossians we are advised to let our speech be always with grace seasoned with salt in order to know how to answer every man. In Ephesians, we are commanded to speak the truth in love. Many verses in Proverbs are delightful about our speaking. Proverbs 25:11 has been often quoted and penned on walls: "A word fitly spoken is like apples of gold in pictures of silver." Proverbs 17:27,28 has taught me to practice keeping my mouth shut. "He that hath knowledge spareth his words: and a man of understanding is of an excellent spirit. Even a fool, when he holdeth his peace, is counted wise: and he that shutteth his lips is esteemed a man of understand." Someone paraphrased that last part: "It's better to keep your mouth shut and let folks think you are a fool than to open it and remove all doubt."

But we do speak, as did Christ, Who is called "The Word of God." [John 1:1,14; Revelation 19:13]. When men heard Him speak, change was brought into their lives. Two temple guards were sent to capture Him and bring Him to the council. They went to where He was speaking, heard Him and returned without Him. When asked why they had failed to bring Him, their only answer was: "Never man spake like this man." [John 7:46]. True. No man ever spoke, lived, loved, or died like this Man. He left us some examples as to how to speak. In so doing, folks will recognize that we belong to Him.

In Luke 4, His very first message is recorded. Verse 22 describes His speaking: "All bare him witness, and wondered at the gracious words which proceeded out of his moth. And they all said, 'Is not this Joseph's son?'" They did not expect one from that family to speak as He did. Folks may be surprised, knowing our background, to hear the things we say that are gracious in the hearing of God and of men. Two things led up to that sort of speaking. They are revealed by John.

In John 3:34, as John declares that he is not the Messiah, he goes on to describe Messiah's speech. "For He whom God hath sent speaketh the words of God: for God giveth not the Spirit by measure unto him." Christ was emptied of all self and sin, thus able to receive all of the Holy Spirit in an unlimited way. Sin in our lives limits the fullness of the Holy Spirit in our lives. Being so filled, Christ was able to clearly, fully, speak the words of God, which are inspired by the Holy Spirit.

Speaking in such a manner, Spirit filled, and just the words of God, caused Jesus to declare in John 6:63, "It is the Spirit that quickeneth; the flesh profiteth nothing: the words that I speak unto you, they are spirit, and they are life." Peter responded in verse 68, "Thou hast the words of eternal life."

On at least one occasion, as He had finished speaking, the Scriptures record: "And the common people heard Him gladly." [Mark 12:37]. His gracious, Spirit led, God honoring speaking must have been simple and down on the level of those who were listening. May our speech ever be so.

In America, one need not go far to find himself in a crowd where various things are spoken, causing us to quickly and readily identify the origin of the speaker. We may not understand a word that is spoken, but his speech makes his origin clear. In later years, that same Peter, preaching to the Jewish Sanhedrin, finished his message with a statement that only this Christ could save. There must have been some snickering at the way he spoke, but when he was done, this was stated of him and John his companion: "Now when they saw the boldness of Peter and John, and perceived that they were unlearned and ignorant men, they marvelled; and then they took knowledge of them, that they had been with Jesus." [Acts 4:13]. There was never a doubt but that, by their speech, they clearly belonged to Jesus.

Your speech betrays you. What is it telling the world in which you live?

16 Entangled Again

When I first tried this art of heading and heeling, the first thing I learned was a lot of jokes. For example: "You can always tell a header or heeler by how many fingers he has left on his hand!" Well meaning men explained that if you did not dally right, you stood the chance of losing a finger, usually a thumb, as you got caught in the rope. There is a grave spiritual danger as well in being caught up, or entangled.

In writing to the church of Galatia, at chapter 5, verse one, Paul wrote: "and be not entangled again with a yoke of bondage." You had been entangled, were set free and now were in danger of being entangled again. Don't do that! The danger was that there were those who wanted to add to the finished work of Jesus Christ. To them, it was not "saved by grace through faith," note verses 4-6; but it was "saved by Christ," plus keeping the law, i.e. being circumcised, supposedly dealt with back in Acts 15.

Gentiles were being saved by the grace of God and though the saved Jews were thrilled by it, there were those who sincerely, in error, believed that they needed to be circumcised – like a good Jew! The

Council's decision was a unanimous "No." There is nothing you can add to what Christ did for us on the Cross of Calvary. And the cross is the issue, note verse eleven of Galatians five. "Then is the offense of the cross ceased."

This sort of battle is an unbearable yoke. Peter stated that to the Council. "Now therefore, why tempt ye God, to put a yoke upon the neck of the disciples, which neither our fathers nor we were able to bear?" [Acts 15:10]. Having to address the issue again in Galatians makes it clear that it was also an ongoing battle, entangled again. There were only about twelve years difference between the writing of Galatians and the writing of Acts; but many years had transpired from the founding of the Church Universal in Acts to the founding of the local Church of Galatia. The problem had not gone away.

This matter of adding to the finished work of Christ is seen in many areas other than a demand for circumcision. Being baptized is a vital part of a believer's life for it indicates obedience to the command of Christ; and is a testimony to one's death, burial, and resurrection with Christ. But it does not wash away the filth of the flesh. Only the blood of Christ could do that. [I Peter 3:21]. There is the consideration of church membership, forms of worship, styles of worship, types of music and the list goes on. The issue here was one of keeping the Law. None of those have to do with the redemption of a lost soul. Salvation is by grace, through faith in Christ alone.

Thus, Paul goes on to state to the church of Galatia that if they add to the finished work, it is a discredit to Christ, "Christ will profit you nothing." Or, as is more strongly stated: "I do not frustrate the grace of God: for if righteousness come by the law, then Christ is dead in vain." [Galatians 2:21]. There is nothing you can do, no law you can keep, no practice you can follow that can add to the salvation that God gave you in Christ. The danger is, if we add anything to the work of Christ, more additions will come. If you must keep one aspect of the law, then you are "a debtor to keep the whole law." [Verse 3]. And don't be deceived, there are not just ten commandments, there are over 1,100 commandments in the Old Testament. You're in for a rough ride!

"Christ is become of no effect unto you." [Galatians 5:4]. These "extras" do not give a stronger bond to Christ, they become a wedge between you and Christ. You will find yourself struggling to maintain the extras rather than resting in Christ and His love for you. He will be driven away by that wedge.

You were running well, what hindered you from obeying the truth? [Verse 7]. In verse eight, it is made clear that this persuasion, to add something to the redemption in Christ, did not come from Him, i.e. God who called you. But you are listening to someone other than God at this point. The danger is made greater as you realize that if you get side-tracked, others will too. Or, perhaps you are off the trail because someone you respected and loved led you off. Paul puts it thus: "A little leaven leaveneth the whole lump." [Verse 9]. True. The leaven in the bread affects the whole loaf. Soon, one individual involved in error leads to a church, a Bible Study Group, involved in error. There is no private belief in this matter, others will be affected.

You may pay a price for believing, for preaching, for standing for Christ alone as your means of redemption, but that is the message of the Cross. You were crucified with Christ. [Galatians 2:20]. On that cross, just the two of you. No one else, nothing else. But on that cross God gave you the gift of life in Christ Who now lives inside of you. You need nobody, nor anything else. Now, go a step further, note verses 13,14 in Galatians 5, "For you, brethren, have been called to liberty; only do not use liberty as an opportunity for the flesh, but through love serve one another. For all the law is fulfilled in one word, even in this, 'You shall love your neighbor as yourself.'" You are free, not to sin, for you are a new creation in Christ. God has freed you that you might serve Him, evidenced by love to your neighbor. As you serve, don't be entangled again.

69

17 Facing Prejudice

In John 7:7, Christ made a contrast by stating: "The world cannot hate you; but me it hateth, because I testify of it, that the works thereof are evil." Yet He warned in Matthew 5:11 that we would be reviled, and in John 17:14 told the Father in prayer that "the world hath hated them."

Peter understood the theme well and wrote in I Peter 2:2 and 3:16 that the world would speak evil of us and that we should not be surprised when we are persecuted [I Peter 4:12] and we were not to be ashamed. [I Peter 4:16]. Though we should not be surprised when the world speaks evil of us, perhaps a greater concern should be what is recorded in Luke 6:26, "Woe unto you, when all men shall speak well of you! For so did their fathers to the false prophets." If you live godly, the prejudice of men will bring you into suffering and persecution. You won't have to hunt for it or work for it, just live godly and it will be there.

Prejudice is "a preconceived and unreasonable judgment or opinion, usually an unfavorable one marked by suspicion, fear, intolerance or hatred." (New World Dictionary, Second College Edition). We hesitate to accept that which is different, especially in an individual, be it nationality, disease, dwarfism/giantism, a limb missing, mute, deaf, blind, and, of grave concern in the world: color. This was seen in the lives of the black cowboys in the early years of the cattle industry. African American cowhands worked side by side with the vaqueros and Anglo cowboys.

With them they were poorly fed, underpaid, overworked, choked in dust, suffered broken bones and spills from horses. Besides that, the African American Cowboy had to survive discrimination, bigotry, and prejudice. Thus, many strove to be the best, just to be accepted, at roping, bronc riding, working with cattle. So wrote Sara R. Massey in her book: "Black Cowboys of America." And some were the best, though never recognized at the time.

Bill Pickett from Taylor, Texas, 1870 to 1932, rode with the 101 Ranch Show and invented the art of bulldogging, now better known as steer wrestling. Cowdogs of the bulldog breed subdued cattle by biting the lips of the animal. Bill Pickett used to drop from the back of his saddle horse, Spradley, grab the steer by the horns, twist his nose upward and grab the lip with his teeth, then drop the steer to the ground. Others tried it as well, but he invented it. Among his close friends were Will Rogers and Tom Mix. He was deeply respected by those of the 101 Ranch and all cowboys who knew him, yet because he was black he was banned from competing with white rodeo contestants. He may have been one of the greatest record setters in rodeo. He was killed by being kicked in the head by a horse in 1932.

Jesse Stahl, in the early 1900's competed in an Oregon rodeo, made an extraordinary ride and was awarded only second place – because of his color. On his next ride, to protest the judges' decision, he rode his bronc facing backwards and carrying a suitcase in his hand. He was a rider!

Bose Ikard rode with Oliver Loving and Charles Goodnight on the "Goodnight Loving Cattle Trail." Goodnight wrote of him: "Bose surpassed any man I had in endurance and stamina. There was a dignity, a cleanliness and reliability about him that was wonderful. His behavior was very good in a fight (with Comanches or outlaws) and he was probably the most devoted man to me that I ever knew. I have trusted him farther than any man. "When we carried money, I gave it to Bose, for a thief would never think of robbing him." On Bose's grave stone, Charles Goodnight had engraved, in part, "never shirked a duty or disobeyed an order…splendid behavior."

With the African American Cowboy, the real difference was not the outside, but the inside. He had something more than his white companions, he had melanin. Melanin is the only true skin coloring. The more you have the darker you are. It is actually that simple. It's what he had inside! So too with the believer. He has something, i.e. Someone inside that the world does not have. Someone that changes his life and makes him different. Christ had that Someone without measure. [Acts 10:38]. That Someone is the Holy Spirit of God. He, being within us, changes our outward actions and very appearance and brings out the hatred, the prejudice of the world. The cowboy, or cowgirl for that matter, can come in any color. Color, or the lack of it, does not make you a cowboy, nor does gender.

But color and gender has often paid a price due to the prejudice of those who feared what was different. We are all of one blood. [Acts 17:26]. There are no "races," as some would like us to believe.

We, as we are, have been chosen by Christ and ordained to spread the gospel. [John 15:16; 17:18]. When we stand at the Judgment Seat of Christ, if there is a word of praise for us, it will be "well done, good and faithful servant." Serving has nothing to do with color or gender. It has everything to do with being good, i.e. godly, and faithful. "Moreover it is required in stewards, that a man be found faithful." [I Corinthians 4:2]. How did we make the ride?

As Christ was ending the final Passover supper with His disciples, He encouraged their hearts with these words: "These things I have spoken unto you, that in me ye might have peace. In the world ye shall have tribulation: but be of good cheer; I have overcome the world." [John 16:33]. And through Christ, so will we.

73

18 Habits of Life

Kristian and I were sitting on the front porch of the ranch house, gazing out across the meadow at the herd of black yearlings there. Our eyes easily went on up the hillside to the beautiful blue sky with its few lazy clouds just hanging up there. I had come over to the Ranch to begin a discipling program with him that evening, and we were enjoying the quiet and the prospect of entering into the study of God's Word. I was surprised to hear him say that in just a short time the herd would all move up the hill to bed down. I asked "Why? Why don't they just stay where they are?" His only reply was that they possibly went up to get a lick of salt before bedding down, but that he really did not know why. He just knew that every evening, without fail, every one of the herd would go up to the hilltop to bed down. They had this habit.

In the 1800's, Samuel Smiles wrote this about habits:

"Sow a thought, reap an act,

Sow an act, reap a habit,

Sow a habit, reap a character,

75

Sow a character, reap a destiny."

He would have found an echo to that in Jeremiah 6:19, "Hear, O earth! Behold, I will bring evil upon this people, EVEN THE FRUIT OF THEIR THOUGHTS, because they have not hearkened unto My words, nor to My law, but rejected it." (emphasis mine). Sow a thought… reap an act…reap a destiny. Jeremiah's people were a people of sin who continually broke his heart and made him weep. He clearly understood that the things they did started with their thoughts and became the habits of their lives. Sinful habits. We all are creatures of habit. The kind of habit traces back to our thoughts.

When Paul wrote of a spiritual man in I Corinthians 2:15,16, he made an amazing observation. "But he that is spiritual judgeth all things, yet himself is judged of no man. For who hath known the mind of the Lord, that he may instruct Him? But we have the mind of Christ." He was quoting, evidently, from Isaiah 40:13 and applying it to Christ. I did not believe I had the mind of Christ as he stated, had not even considered it. But it made me think. What was the mind of Christ like? What habits did His thinking lead him into? I found three.

The first was recorded in Luke 4:16, "And He came to Nazareth, where He had been brought up: and, as His custom was, He went into the synagogue on the Sabbath day, and stood up for to read." The book of Isaiah was given to him and He read from chapter 61, verses one and two. He closed the book and began to preach. What struck me was that going to the synagogue and reading the Word of God was His custom, that is, His habit of life. It's true that, especially as cowboys in the outdoors, "We can worship God without being in a building." That's true, but it often is a cop out for not going to a fellowship with other believers. Like to church. In Hebrews 10:25, we are warned to not be like others who forsake the assembling of themselves with other believers. And they seem to forget that Christ said that where two or three are gathered together in His name – that's where He would be. In the gathering. Since that was His habit, I wanted it to be mine. And I have never regretted it.

That habit of being in the synagogue, reading the Word, and on that occasion, speaking, developed into further speaking. A second habit. Mark recorded in chapter ten and verse one: "And He arose from thence, and cometh into the coasts of Judea by the farther side of Jordan: and the people resort unto Him again; and, as He was wont, He taught them again." His custom was to teach. He taught them again. But, you object, I'm not a teacher. You should be. The writer of Hebrews in chapters five and six made it clear that after you are born again, you ought to grow up, be meat eaters, not just milk drinkers. And, be teachers. [Hebrews 5:12-14]. There is someone you can reach that no one else can reach. Each of us has a mission field of our own. Usually on our own doorstep. Sitting on that horse beside you. Maybe your header or heeler. There is someone who will listen to you share your testimony, quote a verse of Scripture, tell what Christ means to you, who would never listen to anyone else. You have bought into his life. He will buy into yours and hear. Teach.

A third habit led to His captivity. But it did not stop Him from going to the place. Luke 22:39, "And He came out (of the Upper Room), and went, as He was wont, to the Mount of Olives; and His disciples also followed Him." Verse 40 adds in part: "When He was at the place…" The place was the Garden of Gethsemane at the foot of that mount. John 18:1-2 add this to the occasion: "When Jesus had spoken these words, He went forth with His disciples over the brook Cedron, where was a garden, into the which He entered, and His disciples. And Judas also, which betrayed Him, knew the place: for Jesus ofttimes resorted thither with His disciples." Judas knew the place. He knew the habit. And Christ knew that he knew and would arrive soon to betray Him. But He went there anyhow. That garden was His place of prayer and fellowship with God. Prayer was where He talked things over with God, poured out His heart, pled for His people, surrendered to do the will of God. Though it would cost Him betrayal, suffering and death, He would be there. Prayer meant more to Jesus Christ than anything else in His personal makeup. It was His habit. I wanted it to be mine. At any cost. "Sow a thought, reap an act; sow an act, reap a habit…" What are you thinking… now?

19 Women, Beyond the Normal

The slogans on the sweatshirts worn by two cowgirls caught my eye. One read: "Some of the best cowboys I know are cowgirls!" The other, showing a girl on a running horse, read: "If you can't keep up with the girls, stay at home with the boys." On roundups in New Mexico and Wisconsin, I have ridden with some of the girls of that caliber. They can ride, rope, head, heel, and work cattle with the best of the cowboys. Yet, those I worked with were always ladies. They were just a bit beyond the normal.

At an enactment of a "Buffalo Bill's Wild West Show," I was intrigued by the young woman portraying the legend, Annie Oakley. She was good. We all were delighted with her riding and shooting skills. Annie Oakley, an Ohio girl, stood but five feet tall and weighed but 110 pounds when mature. She not only enjoyed her skills, being competent beyond most men, but longed "to see every woman know how to handle firearms as naturally as they knew how to handle babies." She taught many to do so. In a skill usually dominated by men, she won, yet it is recorded of her in history that she was also admired for her refined, ladylike manner.

We owe a lot to the women who have made a mark in a world which often seemed dominated by men. And yet remained ladies, as God intended them to be. The same holds true in the world of godliness and Christianity. There are women who stood out for God then and stand out for God today.

I think of Deborah, the warrior woman, recorded in Judges 4 and 5. She was willing to face the foe at the side of Barak who would not face them alone. Ruth the Moabitess, who bore the loss of her husband and went on to care for her embittered mother in law. Rahab the harlot, who faced death by hiding the two spies from Joshua's army. A few of many from the Old Testament. In the New Testament, there is Mary Magdalene, from whom Christ cast out seven demons. Priscilla, who with her husband, Aquila, ministered to Paul and, "laid down their own necks" for him. Phebe, who served and labored in a church in Cenchrea. The lists goes on.

And there was Mary. Mary, the virgin wife of Joseph, who became the mother of Jesus. As a cowboy, I find it easy to lovingly and respectfully think of her as "The Woman in the Stable."

To our knowledge, she never explained her conception of Jesus, as a virgin, not having known a man. What was true in Luke 2:19 seemed to stay true of her throughout her life. "But Mary kept all these things, and pondered them in her heart." She had gone through the period when Joseph was "minded to put her away." [Matthew 1:19]. From all appearances she had been unfaithful. I see in Mary a woman with such love for God that she was willing to lose the love of Joseph. She would also lose the respect of the community. Nazareth wasn't that big of a town! Beyond that, she stood to lose her very life, for stoning to death was the penalty for such immorality. She stayed true to her calling. God exonerated her. And we are the blessed of God through the Son she bore.

Besides her willingness to lose so much for God, Mary was willing to face loneliness. She could have been alone, without Joseph, unwanted by any other man. In Luke's record of the birth of Christ it is clear that she brought forth Jesus. She wrapped Him in swaddling clothes. She placed Him in the manger. She? Where was Joseph? In fact, where was anybody? In defense of Joseph, it is possible that when the birth pains began, he went out in search of an apothecary or a mid-wife to come help. While he was gone, the baby came. It is evident that no one saw God's Son come into the world. (I recall that, at the cross, great darkness covered the land. No one saw God's Son leave the world.) She, alone, was directing the meal at the marriage in Cana of Galilee. Willing to be lonely in order to bring glory to God alone. And never a recorded word of complaint.

She also was loyal. Can you see her there at the cross? All those who stood there that day were putting their lives on the line. They certainly were putting their relationship with the leaders of the Synagogues in jeopardy. "Now there stood by the cross of Jesus, His mother." [John 19:25]. With her stood Mary the wife of Cleophas and Mary Magdalene. One man is mentioned, though not by name. We know it was John because he is called "the beloved disciple." But where were the other ten? Judas had committed suicide. Women stood where men should have been. They would be the ones as well who would be first at the empty tomb. First to tell the story of the resurrection, only to be disbelieved. But to be proven true by Christ Himself. Women who went beyond the normal and made a difference in their world.

Where would you have been that day? With the men, or with the women?

20 The Greatest Verse in the Bible

The cover of the April, 2008 Western Horseman magazine, was an eye catcher, showing Chance O'Neal on Sixes Pick. The caption was: "The World's Greatest Ranch Horse: Chance O'Neal rides 'Sixes Pick' to a historic championship." The word "greatest" brought to mind a statement I had heard more than sixty years ago.

Since I was a child, I have heard that word, greatest, used of boxers, runners, race-car drivers, explorers, scientists, buildings, automobiles. About anything you can think of has had the word greatest used of some item or person in that field.

That word was used while I was sitting in the little Baptist Church where I had previously given my life to Christ and been born again. The speaker was an evangelist, scheduled to be there for a week and speak ten times. He quoted John 3:16 from the old King James translation: "For God so loved the world that He gave His only begotten Son, that whosoever believeth in Him should not perish but have everlasting life." He then stated: "This is the greatest verse in all of the Bible." And he preached on just that one verse for all ten messages. He never repeated a thing he had said in a previous message, but just kept expounding the truths from that verse. I could not believe there was THAT MUCH in so few words. But it was there.

The years have gone by, new translations of the Bible have come, new philosophies of life have been set forth, change seems to have come all over. But John 3:16 still remains as the dearest verse in all of the Bible, sort of summing up everything that is in the book. I have long forgotten all that the evangelist said so long ago, but I find it easy to turn to the verse and agree as to its greatness. For instance:

"For God," reveals the Greatest Planner. In Hebrews, we read that the works of God were finished from the foundation of the world. In Revelation, we read of the Lamb slain from the foundation of the world. Christ came in the fullness of time, we are told. How amazing to realize that the Creator, even while bringing into existence the world in which we live, was also planning the redemption and the Redeemer that we would need. His plan has been flawlessly unfolded from that beginning.

"So Loved," the Greatest Passion. Jeremiah first recorded that God loved us with an everlasting love, and John backs that up revealing that Jesus, having loved His own that were in the world, loved them to the very end. In Romans, Paul makes it clear that this love came to us, not that we deserved it, but it came while we were yet sinners. That love is so great that in Christ's High Priestly prayer of John 17 He made it clear that God the Father loved us as much as He loved Christ. That's hard to fathom!

"The World," the Greatest Population. Not just some selected few, but the WORLD! And that's why Christ could proclaim, "Whosoever will, let him come!" As He talked with Nicodemus, Christ made it clear that He had not come to condemn the world, but that the world, through Him, might be saved. He later, when talking to the multitudes, made it clear that all that the Father gave Him would come to Him, and that those who came would never be cast out. Only those who receive Him will be saved, but the love of God was for the whole world.

"He gave," the Greatest Present. In John 4:10, called "the gift of

God." In Romans 5:15, the gift is called "the free gift." No way you can buy it; no way do we deserve it. Free. But it must be received as John told us in the first chapter of the book which bears his name. "To as many as received Him..." You can look at a gift, admire it and evaluate it, but it's not yours until you take it, receive it. A man could die of starvation at a banquet table if he did not eat of that which was provided. A man can die and go to hell if he does not receive the gift of eternal life in Christ which God has provided.

"His only begotten Son," the Greatest Person. No other man in history has marked and changed the world as Jesus Christ of Nazareth has. And, still is doing in countries around the world. Of Him, God could say: "This is my beloved Son, in Whom I am well pleased." [Matthew 17:5]. No one could convince Him of sin. No one could improve on what He had to say. There never was a greater lover of sinful mankind. Only He could declare that all God had asked Him to do, He had finished.

"That Whosoever," the Greatest Privilege. You. Me. Whosoever. Enabled to be born into the family of the God of gods and Lord of lords. To be called a son of God and to have a place prepared for eternity. Never to have our sins of the past brought before us since they were cleansed in the blood of the Lamb. God did that for whosoever. No one eliminated who would take the next step, which is:

"Believeth," the Greatest Profession. We believe with our hearts, we confess Christ as Lord with our mouths. That's the way Paul put it to the Romans. [Romans 10:9, 10]. John recalled the first part, "He that heareth My word, and believeth..." [John 5:24]. Thus it is so important that we who have believed tell the old, old story for others cannot believe in One of Whom they have not heard.

"In Him," the Greatest Payment. The Matchless, Sinless, Son of God. As a gospel chorus states: We had a debt we could not pay, He paid a debt He did not owe. Thank You, Jesus. Just to think that God counted us worth Calvary.

"Should not Perish," the Greatest Preservation. Though the body may be placed in the ground, awaiting its resurrection, the real person, the spirit-soul will never die but has everlasting life. And in God's due time that old body will be resurrected and a new body be given to the redeemed.

"But Have," the Greatest Possession. All other things are "but loss." This answers the question: "For what is a man profited, if he shall gain the whole world, and lose his own soul? Or what shall a man give in exchange for his soul?" [Matthew 16:26]. Nothing is of greater value, nothing worth the exchange. This eternal life in Christ is yours.

"Everlasting Life," the Greatest Permanence. Nothing, no nothing, can separate us from that love and from that life. That was the firm persuasion of Paul in Romans 8:38, 39.

That is the reason John 3:16 is The Greatest Verse in the Bible.

21 Follow the Boss

Matthew 4:18-22 has a few things in it that sound like a cattle drive, and I don't mean that disrespectfully. "And Jesus, walking by the sea of Galilee, saw two brethren, Simon called Peter, and Andrew his brother, casting a net into the sea: for they were fishers. And he saith unto them, 'Follow me, and I will make you fishers of men.' And they straightway left their nets, and followed him. And going on from thence, he saw other two brethren, James the son of Zebedee, and John his brother, in a ship with Zebedee their father, mending their nets; and he called them. And they immediately left the ship and their father, and followed him."

When called to help drive cattle, and told to be there at 6:00 A.M., you don't pull in at 6:00 A.M. (or, later!). By the appointed time you have already arrived, are tacked up and ready to step into the leather the moment the Boss cries out to "Mount up." He wants you to be prompt. Notice that same thing in verses 20 and 22. The word is "immediately," both times.

Your position is to follow. [Verse19]. Always true of your position on a cattle drive. You follow the Boss. It is never cowboy etiquette to ride

87

ahead of the Boss. And at the same time, never to give orders or tell him how to work cattle and get things done. We don't give orders, we just report for duty. On the drive, once the cattle are gathered, there are three possible positions on which you can ride: Point, or Lead, Flank or Wing, Drag or Tail. Pick the Drag. Nobody much wants that position anyhow. Recall the story Christ told of being invited to a feast. He made it clear that when you arrived, take a lower seat. If you take a higher seat, there is always a possibility that someone "greater" than you might show up and you will be asked to vacate your chosen high seat for this newly arrived guest. Embarrassing! Take a low seat, and, perhaps, you will hear the host say, "Friend, come up higher." Joy! The Boss will appoint your position, but don't put yourself on top.

Follow Me...Christ...the "Boss," that's the Person to follow. An animal with two heads is a freak and will not live. There can't be two heads on a drive, nor two heads in your spiritual life. Take time to read Mark 9:38-41 where John is upset because he with other disciples had seen a man casting out demons in Jesus' name and forbade him "because he does not follow us." "Follow Us?" When did that become the main issue? On a drive, you follow the Boss and his instructions. In the life of the Christian you follow Christ, He is the "Me," in the invitation. The Person is not the denomination, the prayer group, the Bible study group. It is Christ. We follow Him and get our instructions from Him. Him alone!

When you proceed on this thought in the Bible, you discover that to follow Christ, a price is paid. The disciples made it clear that they were concerned that they had "left all" to follow Him. [Mathew 19:27,28]. You can't follow if you are holding on to something. Or someone. Paul summed up the surrender by counting all things but "dung," refuse, in order to follow Christ. Salvation cost you nothing. As a precious old hymn states it: "Jesus paid it all, all to Him I owe, sin had left a crimson stain, He washed it white as snow." There is no price, no cost to be saved. To serve Him will cost you all that you have. And it may hurt. In cowboying, there is not a question of paying a price, of whether or not you will get hurt, but rather of when and how bad! The price is just part of the life. Christ encouraged their hearts by letting them know that the reward is up ahead. You will sit on twelve thrones. You will never walk in darkness. These are the real times to cowboy up and not whine or criticize.

The biggest danger, peril, on the walk with Christ, or on the drive, is to get too far behind. Peter did that and it cost him more than he would have dreamed. "But Peter followed him afar off unto the high priest's palace, and went in, and sat with the servants, to see the end." [Matthew 26:58].

Before long he was swearing profanely and denying the very One Whom he had vowed to die with if need be. Instead of taking a stand and, as we might say, "Riding for the brand," he denied the outfit completely. He was following, but a long ways back. Of no value. With no strength to be true. Headed for tears and regret which he would remember for the rest of his life.

Cowboys are quite independent. Of course you are aware of that. So too, following Christ, the Boss, is a very independent matter. Once Peter and Christ were reconciled, the command was given again, "follow Me." [John 21:20-23]. For some reason, Peter turned around, having caught a glimpse of John, and asked Christ, "But Lord, what about this man?" Christ's reply was quite polite as He stated: "If I will that he remain till I come, what is that to you?" We might have said, with less love and concern: "That's none of your business." And it really isn't! The call is completely personal. You, follow Me! In doing so, you will have enough to handle in life. Don't worry about the other man - that's between him and Christ. This, the call of God on your life, that is your affair. Follow Me!

22 Designed for Fruitfulness

In Matthew 13:24-30, Jesus is giving a second parable of seed planting and fruitfulness, in order to describe the working of the Kingdom of Heaven. The design is for good seed to be planted and a good crop to be harvested. The surprise was that as the grain matured, it was discovered that weeds had been planted in the field, tares, and that they were growing right beside the wheat. Shall we tear them out? No, let both grow until the harvest, then the weeds will be gathered out and burned. The gain we want will not be greatly hindered by the weeds in the field. The loss by tearing out the weeds now would be greater than the loss by letting them grow with the wheat.

While doing some research on the cattle industry, I saw so much that were parallels to this parable and its explanation in Matthew 13: 37-43. I was surprised to be informed that there are 95 million cattle and calves in the United States. 78% of those are beef cattle. Raised for profit, one of the strange things is that there is a $400 million dollar loss to the industry because of worms, parasites in the cattle. A problem to be constantly dealt with.

Cattle must have good nutrition to start with, and then proper implants to augment what has already been gained by the nutrition. With that combination, you can expect a 4 to 8 percent increase in sucking calves, a 10 to 20 percent increase in growing calves, and a 15 percent increase in finishing cattle. Plus, it has been discovered that cattle grow better in groups than as individuals. An 800 pound steer can enter a feedlot, consume 5,000 pounds of feed and gain 600 pounds of weight in a six month period.

This is enhanced if aerated water, with more oxygen content, is available for consumption. A one-third pound daily weight gain can be anticipated.

Growth can be hindered, however, by aggressive stock in the group, and even by nervous stock in the group. Hindered, but not stopped. Great gains can yet be had.

The man who sowed, sowed good seed. No rancher starts with culls and adds a cull bull to build his herd. So God started with good seed, Adam and Eve without a flaw in their lives. In that sense, just like Him. The Son of Man, Jesus, has sown the sons of the kingdom in the world. Satan has sown his seed as well, the sons of the wicked one. And, it was done "while men slept." Unexpectedly, quietly, while normal processes were going on. But one morning it was a shocking experience to awaken and discover the weeds in the field. Time had gone by, quickly, quietly, and the field was infested. Parasites. Like cattle with worms and other devastating parasites.

The "sons of the kingdom" will also have a battle with parasites. False doctrine, selecting only portions of the Scriptures as inspired. Making scriptures only symbolical. The Ten Commandments are reduced to ten suggestions. We find too many shepherds are really wolves in sheep's clothing. Standards of holiness are gone.

Water has in the Scriptures been used to refer to the Word of God. John 15:3, "Now ye are clean through the word which I have spoken unto you." Titus 3:5, "Not by works of righteousness which we have done, but according to his mercy he saved us, by the washing of regeneration, and renewing of the Holy Ghost." The pure, fresh, oxygenated water of God's Word, taken in ample proportions, always available, will add to our "gain" in the kingdom.

We have no problem acknowledging that there are aggressive, worrisome folks in the kingdom who are a constant hindrance and challenge. The church has always had its problem people in it. Paul wrote to the church at Corinth and stated: "For it hath been declared unto me of you, my brethren, by them which are of the houe of Chloe, that there are contentions among you." [I Corinthians 1:11]. Timothy had a problem with those who despised his youth. John had to face Diotrephes. Peter cautioned us to not be surprised by the fiery trial which would try us. Aggressions are to be expected. Not hunted up, by the way. And the growth continues in spite of it because God has intended the all things of life, to do one basic thing, conform us to the image of Christ. [Romans 8:29]. That's one of the reasons that James states: "My brethren, count it all joy when you fall into diverse temptations." [James 1:2]. You are still going to grow, the gain is still going to come. God intended it that way.

The best thing is that God, too, uses implants. The Psalmist wrote that he had hidden God's Word in his heart so that he might not sin against God. Christ has asked the Father, and the request was granted, that He would send the Holy Spirit into our lives to guide us into all truth, to bring us comfort, and reveal Christ more clearly to us. Then, He plants us into a fellowship of believers and plants in us a love and oneness for and with them. Growth is always the result. Fruit will be the evidence.

By their fruit ye shall know them. And, as the parable makes clear, when there is no fruit, the growth evidences that what we are observing is only a weed. In cattle, we look for gain. In the believer, the distinction is the fruit.

23 The Classroom of the Calves

We had experienced the worst winter in the history of our State. How good it was to be able to be out riding again. In just a few weeks, as the green grass began to appear, there was also a noticeable amount of small black spots observed on the ground. The black angus calves had started to arrive on the ranch where it was my privilege to exercise my horses. Sometimes new life is black. Psalm 65, verses 9-13 describes the springtime so beautifully. I love the phrase, "the pastures are clothed with flocks." Isn't that precious, "clothed" with the flocks? And the conclusion is: "They shout for joy, they also sing." You may not be able to carry a tune, but such a sight sure stirs up a song in the heart.

I took time to again thank the rancher for the privilege I had of riding in his pasture and assured him that I would do nothing to disturb his cattle. Never had I seen a quieter herd than he had. He assured me that he would not have a mean, nervous cow on his place. Then, with a big grin, he told me to ride in among them and let them see a horse – for his herd was not worked with horses and the calves had never seen one. So I did. And it got me to thinking. I began to ride out to the herd, slowly ride among them, and let them teach me things of the Lord.

Nine months earlier, those calves had been a combination of a sperm and egg, a combination so small that without a microscope it would be difficult if not impossible to detect. Then, hidden in a dark womb for nine months, growth would take place until they were introduced into the world in which they were ordained to live. The Mexican phrase for birth is so descriptive: "dar a luz." To give to light. Out of that darkness into the light of life. So much like the believer, living so long in the darkness of sin, then, by the grace of God to be born to walk in the light.

We talk about being born again, and think of it as an instantaneous act. In some cases it may be so. In my own life it was not. There was a time when I longed to own a Bible. Got one, put it away, and never read it, but there had been that longing. Then, after a serious auto accident, I felt I ought to thank "Someone," God? I just did not know Him, where He was, how to get in touch. That moment too passed. But there had been another tugging. The day came when I heard the Gospel clearly, but deliberately hardened my heart to it – but only for a week. Then next time I heard it, the birth took place. Years had gone by from the first tug. So too I have prayed for as long as forty years for a particular loved one to get saved and then saw it happen. Don't give up. The birthing will come.

Those calves also taught me a lesson of life. They sure knew where to find the food supply, and often resorted there. Peter described a newborn child of God as being a baby, hungering for the milk of the Word. [I Peter 2:2]. That hunger, and satisfying of it, would lead to growth. Just like the calf. When I find professors of Christianity who do not hunger for God's Word, I question their life in Christ. How's your hunger?

And how inquisitive. One day as I was quietly sitting on the horse, just enjoying the day and watching the herd, I felt my horse turning. Glancing his way, I noted several calves, about six, had begun to come to us and were, from the back starting to surround us. We probably did look queer to them. They wanted to know. Did you ever note in the Exodus that when God appeared to Moses in the burning bush, that He did not speak to Moses until Moses turned aside to see the bush? It was when God observed Moses turning aside to see, to learn, to do something a little extra, that He spoke to him. Jesus would one day say: "Search the Scriptures; for in them ye think ye have eternal life..." [John 5:39]. God loves a curious, inquisitive believer and is always ready to give something extra to the one who will take the time to look, to inquire, to search, to try and find out. He must have a special love for His child with the hungering, inquisitive heart. What on earth is God doing? I'm going to get in step and find out!

Did you notice the nurse cow (which sometimes is a nurse steer!)? There she stands, or, perhaps is lying down, but all around her are a dozen calves. Her responsibility for a while. The herd seems to take turns at baby-sitting. When Jesus confronted Peter after all night of fish-less fishing, He challenged Peter's love for Him. When Peter affirmed that love three times, Christ gave him three commands to fulfill. The first was a surprise. Most folks think Christ said, "feed My sheep." Not so. The first order was to "feed My lambs." [John 21:15]. Far too often a person turns to Christ for salvation, and no one seems to notice or care after the first few minutes of rejoicing. One of the greatest failures of the church is the failure to disciple the new converts. We need some nurse cows. Or steers. Someone to be there to protect, to care, to teach, to come alongside until that new baby is able to walk on its own. Is it possible that the common cow has more sense than the consecrated Christian?

Which made me realize that they all took time to rest. In the Old Testament the command had been to observe the Sabbath. A day of rest. Worship entered it, but the day was a day of rest, a commemoration of God's rest after creating His world. Christ valued rest. Hear Him saying: "Come ye apart and rest awhile." [Matthew 11:28-30; Mark 6:31,32]. The great Southern Baptist pastor, Dr. Vance Havner, used to say: "Come apart and rest, before you come apart!" That quiet time with the Lord! Just Him and you. Keep your Bible handy, He will have something special to say to you.

97

Sometimes, the classroom of the calves is so meaningful, that I just hate to ride back home.

24 Keep it Clean

One of my privileges is to work with 4-H clubs, coaching Mounted Drill Teams. Early in my relationship, I noticed how often youth were riding saddles which appeared to not have been cleaned and oiled since Noah's ark. My bringing this to the attention of our director just ended up with me being given an added responsibility – teach them how to clean them. So much for complaining. This led me to some research, so as to appear to be credentialed to do such teaching.

The old time cowboys traditionally cleaned and oiled their saddles prior to the spring work, and, again, after the fall work was ended. The five enemies of leather they knew were sweat, dirt, humidity, heat and mold. Sweat buildup is a breeding place for mold spores. They used a mixture of alcohol and water to clean up the mold. Today, a mixture of chlorox and water (one tablespoon to a gallon) does the job.

Then, good old neatsfoot oil was applied. The name came from the old, archaic, English word "neat," a term for oxen. Oil from the shin bones of the oxen was used for cleaning leather, hence: "Neats-foot."

Though a good oil, it tends to darken leather. One might use instead such supplies as Leather New, Tee See Leather Oil, Lexol, or Lederbalsam. A clean saddle increases its looks, value and longevity. Quite like a Christian. We too have enemies which tend to destroy us and our usefulness. Three in particular.

The world, the flesh and the Devil have been here from day one of Creation. The coming of Christ was not only to satisfy God's requirements for the redemption of mankind, but also to bring to an end the power those three subjects had over a believer's life. Multiple verses about each subject are well worth investigating for a greater life of victory. Consider just a few.

The world: John wrote of it in sobering terms in I John 2:15 – 17. First of all, don't love the world (system). If you do, you declare that the love of the Father is not in you. No argument! There are three things in the world system which constitute the only three types of sin in the world. Eve faced them in Eden. Christ faced them on the mount of temptation. They are: the lust of the flesh, the lust of the eyes and the pride of life. With Eve, she was tempted to EAT the fruit which she SAW, in order to be WISE like God. That was a challenge to her pride. With Christ, He was tempted to turn the stones into BREAD, own all the KINGDOMS of the WORLD, and show off His care by angels (PRIDE) by casting Himself down from the wall. Your temptations are exactly the same. Make a list of sins, they all fit under one of those three categories. We need to be clean, rid of them. If you confess your sins, God is faithful and just to forgive you and to cleanse you from all unrighteousness. [I John 1:9].

The flesh: Keep in mind that the flesh, the body, was never saved. It is still in the groaning stage awaiting the final redemption in Christ. [Romans 8:23]. The flesh is understood in the five senses we have, which so easily become doorways through which sin enters into our lives, even as saints: touch, taste, smell, sight and hearing. Because of these doorways, a multitude of sins enter into a life to defile it. In Galatians 5:19-21, a long list of such sins is recorded: "Now the works of the flesh are manifest…adultery, fornication, uncleanness, lasciviousness, idolatry, witchcraft, hatred, variance, emulations, wrath, strife, seditions, heresies, envyings, murders, drunkenness, revellings, and such like."

Can anyone plead "Not guilty?" Anyone who does not need cleaned up in some area? Something hidden? I had to make the 4-H group conscious of the fact that you cleaned UNDER the skirts and BEHIND the fenders on the stirrup straps. You might even have to loosen a few screws, saddle strings and remove some conchos to get to the dirt. It all had to go. And it would take work and perseverance.

It does with us as well. That which is secret and hidden to the eyes of men are open and naked in the eyes of God. [Hebrews 4:13]. Get rid of it.

The Devil: First of all, he is real, not just an influence, not an "it." One of God's earliest creations, meant to be close to the Triune God, but was rejected and removed from his privileged place by his pride. One of his chief ways of getting at God, is to attack God's children. He loves to harden and blind the minds of Jews [II Corinthians 3:14], Gentiles [II Corinthians 4: 4], and the church [II Corinthians 11:3]. You fit in one of those categories, and you face that problem.

In James 4:4-8, acknowledging the battle, we are challenged. "Ye adulterers and adulteresses (his titles for those who are defiled by the world) know ye not that the friendship of the world is enmity with God? Whosoever therefore will be a friend of the world is the enemy of God. Do ye think that the Scripture saith in vain, 'The spirit that dwelleth in us lusteth to envy?' But He giveth more grace. Wherefore He saith, 'God resisteth the proud, but giveth grace unto the humble.' Submit yourselves therefore unto God. Resist the devil, and he will flee from you. Draw night to God, and He will draw nigh to you. Cleanse your hands, ye sinners; and purify your hearts, ye double-minded."

Peter warns us that Satan comes as a roaring lion, seeking whom he may devour. He so moves among the brethren throughout the world. We are all in the same battle, all prone to be defiled and have dirt-laden lives. Again we are challenged to resist him, be steadfast in the faith, and enjoy God's victories. [I Peter 5:8, 9]. Keep it clean! Learn to pray with the Psalm writer: "Search me, O God, and know my heart: try me, and know my thoughts: and see if there be any wicked way in me, and lead me in the way everlasting." [Psalm 139:23,24].

25 What's on the Tombstone?

You need to take the time to read Hebrews 11:32-38, for that is the theme for today. Starting with Gideon and ending with an unnamed group who faithfully followed the Lord, God gives us a title which could well have been placed on the tombstone of each individual: "Of whom the world was not worthy." They had so lived for God that nothing, no one in the world, was a match for them in value in the eyes of God. The epitaph says a lot. Some are in jest.

We had been visiting a graveyard in Virginia City, Montana, reading the epitaphs. Some died of natural diseases, some by outlaws, some by vigilantes. We noticed a few – in a separate place that had been written of cowboys, in spoof we believe. For example:

"Here lies old Ben, lanky and skinny. He rustled horses, took one too many."

"In respect to Dennis, he lived fast and loose, slowed down right quick in a hangman's noose."

"Cold was the wind, and hot the sun, Jake was too slow when he pulled his gun."

Good lesson: "Tom: Quite slick of hand, the card he drew, then he got shot, as cheaters do."

All the above in spoof, but there is no joke in the lives of those listed in our text in Hebrews. Consider these: I've added my thoughts of a fitting epitaph.

Gideon: Judges 6-8. Attacked by an innumerable army of Midianites. God cut Gideon's army down from 32,000 to 10,000 to 300 and gave him the victory while God got the glory.

"A few, plus God, was enough."

Barak: Judges 4:1 – 5:21. Partnered with a lady judge, Deborah, because he was afraid to face Sisera and his 900 chariots, fighting for Midian. God sent rain and stopped the chariots, the victory was won, but a woman got the glory.

"He won the battle, but lost the honor."

Samson: Judges 13-16. A miracle birth, a Nazarite vow marked his early life. But he lived in the flesh and only turned to God (for 20 years) when he almost died of dehydration on a battle field. In later years, he again turned to sin, lost his hair, strength, closeness to God. In grace, God allowed the hair to grow again, and he died as he had begun life, as a Nazarite, dedicated to God.

"Grace never fails."

Jephthah: Judges 11,12. Son of a harlot. Kicked out of the family by his legally born brothers. Called back to lead them when under great pressure from a foreign country of Ammonites. He won the victory for them.

"He knew how to forgive, even as God forgives."

David: I Samuel 17. The youngest son of Jesse, not honored at first by his older brothers. He approached Goliath with five stones, because Goliath had three brothers and a father, all giants. He intended to wipe them all out.

"Faithful to the Finish!"

Samuel: I Samuel 3:1,7,21. In his childhood, due to the great sins of the High Priest, Eli, and his godless sons, Hophni and Phinehas, there was no open word from God. God found in Samuel a listening ear, so He began to speak again, and Israel was blessed.

"The man with an open ear and obedient heart.

From that list of names, God goes on to just speak of experiences, but we know of whom He was speaking.

v. 33 Conquered Kingdoms – David

"Preserved of God."

Administered justice – Solomon. Of two harlots, he knew who was the mother of a child.

"God granted his request for wisdom"

Gained what was promised – Joshua. He could state that "Not one thing hath failed of all God promised."

"By Faith he prevailed."

Shut the mouths of lions – who but Daniel!

"Kept by the Lion of the tribe of Judah"

v. 34 Quenched fire – Hananiah, Mishael, Azariah. Called Shadrach, Meshach and Abed-Nego. [Daniel 1:7; Daniel 3].

"Willing to burn out for God."

Peter escaped the edge of the sword in Acts 12.

"Our times are in His hands"

Paul made strong in weakness. [II Corinthians 12:10].

"Not I, but Christ."

v. 35 Women received their dead – Martha and Mary for Lazarus. [John 11].

"We believe in Christ, the Resurrection."

vs. 35, 36 Others were tortured, jeers, floggings, chained, imprisoned

- Paul and Silas, in Acts 16

"They knew the fellowship of His sufferings."

v. 37 Stoned – Stephen. [Acts 7:59].

"He stood on the Rock, Christ Jesus"

Sawed in two - Isaiah [from tradition].

"All, all on the altar laid"

Killed by the sword [James, Acts 12:2].

"Not how long, but how well he lived for Christ."

Destitute, persecuted, mistreated, spoiled of their goods. Saints of God from all over the world in all ages of Christianity. [Hebrews 10:34].

The great summary: "OF WHOM THE WORLD WAS NOT WORTHY."

If your life, right now, were summed up in a sentence, to be placed on your tombstone, what would that sentence read?

What do you wish it would read? You can choose to make it known by a life of surrender.

26 Branded: To Whose Outfit Do You Belong?

In Galatians 6:17, Paul states: "for I bear in my body the marks of the Lord Jesus." He was not referring to what is called "stigmata" in the psychological sense. Those marks some zealots have which are on the wrists, side and feet, similar to the marks on Christ's crucified body. Yet, verses 14-18 are definitely tied to the cross. And the Greek word used here for "marks" is the word "stigma." Other translations are helpful here. The New American Standard, the Amplified New Testament, and the Greek scholar, Wuest, all translate the word: "the brandmarks." The New English Bible uses the phrase: "the marks of Jesus, branded on my body." I believe that the translations of Williams and of Beck catch the meaning best when they translate: "the scars that mark me as Jesus' slave." That is in keeping with the meaning of the Greek word, stigma.

The stigma was a mark incised or punched (pricked) on a person for recognition of ownership. A mark burned in. In the New World Dictionary, Second College Edition, the definition reads: "A distinguishing mark burned or cut into the flesh, as of a slave or criminal." Paul had such marks.

Consider the list in II Corinthians 11:23-33. Paul five times received "forty lashes save one." He was beaten with rods three times. Once he was stoned and taken up from the ground as a dead man. There were three occasions when he was shipwrecked. Besides those outward marks, Paul speaks of his hunger and thirst, his being cold and naked. I've often thought that Dr. Luke was appointed as his companion in order to minister to Paul, to doctor him in those trying times of his life. God knew what he would suffer, as Christ said to Ananias. [Acts 9:16]. They left their marks. He was always easy to spot in a crowd. The scars that mark me as Jesus' slave. Indeed!

The brand denoted the owner, the outfit. To Timothy, Paul wrote: "Nevertheless the foundation of God standeth sure, having this seal, 'The Lord knoweth them that are His.' And, 'Let everywhone that nameth the name of Christ depart from iniquity.'" [II Timothy 2:19]. From the second letter to the church at Corinth, this seal, seen by God, is revealed as being visible to others. [II Corinthians 1:21, 22]. "Now He which establishes us with you in Christ, and hath anointed us, is God; Who hath also sealed us, and given the earnest of the Spirit in our hearts." Somehow the "seal" and the Holy Spirit seem connected. This is verified in Ephesians 1:12,13, "That we should be to the praise of His glory, who first trusted in Christ. In whom ye also trusted, after that ye heard the Word of truth, the Gospel of your salvation: in whom after that ye believed, ye were sealed with that Holy Spirit of promise." God looks for the Holy Spirit in the life of a professor of faith, as the seal that he belongs to Christ. We have that same opportunity and privilege. And that seal, like the brand on our livestock, will last forever. "And grieve not the Holy Spirit of God, whereby ye are sealed unto the day of redemption." [Ephesians 4:30]. That final day of full redemption is yet before us. In the meantime, what is the mark for which we look? Christ said: "You will know them by their fruits." And "Therefore by their fruits you will know them." [Matthew 7:16, 20]. Thus, we need to look for the Fruit of the Spirit as the mark of the Spirit, showing genuine redemption. That mark which shows the ownership of our lives. The fruit is clearly described in Galatians 5:22,23.

Love is a new Constraint. The love of Christ constrains us.

Joy is a new Cheer. There's not much to rejoice about in the world, but there is joy in Jesus.

Peace is a new Condition. Being justified by faith [Romans 5:1] we have peace.

Longsuffering is a new Continuance. Because He put up with us, we can put up with others.

Gentleness (Kindness) is a new Characteristic. God smooths out our life and tongue.

Goodness, depicts a new Character. Only one is good, that is God. He's changing us.

Faith (Faithfulness) is a new Commitment. We don't need to see in order to believe and obey.

Meekness (Gentleness) is a new Contentment. We don't need to defend ourselves. He is there.

Temperance (Self-control) is a new Control. A life run by the Holy Spirit according to God's Word.

Why all the above? Why "new?" Because of the new truth the church at Galatia was learning. "For in Christ Jesus neither circumcision availeth any thing, nor uncircumcision, but a new creature." [Galatians 6:15]. Those who are crucified with Christ, marked, sealed by the Holy Spirit of God, made new, will be visible not only to God, but to the world. On those persons will come peace and mercy. [Galatians 6:16].

You are being watched. Every day. By an unknown, but great mass of people. How do they read you?

How does God?

27 Trust Him, He'll Get You Home

I can still recall Granddad saying those words to me when I was about 12 years old. We had been putting up hay and working corn in Wallace, West Virginia, about ten miles away from the home farm near Lumberport. While Granddad was alive, all we ever had to work with was horses. No tractors or such equipment. How the horses got to Wallace and to the fields I do not know. Probably Granddad rode them there. We had no stock trailer. All I knew now was that he was telling me, early in the morning, to ride the horses back to the farm. I had no idea, at that time, where on earth the farm was. Some basic direction was given to me for the ten mile ride, and as my fears were noticeable, the final direction was this: "When you get to a place and do not know which way to turn, trust Prince (one of the two horses, the other being Nancy) to make the decision. He'll get you home."

Having ridden several hours, I knew I must be getting close to home when I came to a T in the road. And there I had no idea as to which way to turn. First, I faced fear that I'd NEVER get back to the farm. Or, since I was now in the middle of nowhere (I thought) someone would come by and do me harm.

I did not know then that fear was so common, recorded about 400 times in the Bible. Nor did I know that apart from genuine cause for fear, that there was a spirit of fear, coming from the enemy. Paul had told Timothy that God did not give us the spirit of fear, but of power and love and a sound mind. [II Timothy 1:7]. I did not know Christ at the time, and, naturally, did not know the Word of God, but I knew I could trust Granddad. So, by a great act of courage and faith (as a frightened 12 year old), I kicked Prince in the ribs and told him to get up – and let the reins hang. He took a few steps further and turned right. We went about a half mile and he turned left, and suddenly I recognized exactly where I was. What a peace was mine. Granddad simply explained later that Prince would get me home because he knew where the manger was! Horses seldom are lost.

In my years of serving Christ, there have been times when fear has come as uncertainty was before me. I don't know what to do, where to turn. At those times I turn in my heart to John 14, the discourse in the Upper Room. John 14:1-6 records the precious promise of Christ that He was going to go away to prepare a place for us. We like to think of and sing of that place as a "mansion, just over the hilltop." It is more proper to think of it as a room in the Father's house. That He would return was added to the promise. The words that disturbed the disciples, especially Thomas were: "And where I go you know, and the way you know." Thomas made it clear that they did not know where He was going and how could they know the way? The answer was simple. Christ said: "I Am the Way, the Truth, and the Life. No one comes to the Father except through Me." He could have added the words which He first gave to them when he invited them to join Him on the journey: "Follow Me." Those words are still the answer.

Christ knew where He lived. As He prayed in John 17, the real High Priestly prayer, in verses 5 and 24, He spoke to the Father about restoring the glory which He had had with Him before the world was. It was an eternal glory, and now it was time for it to be restored. The work was almost done and He would soon be going home. He knew where He lived and would not get lost on the way back home. Trust Him.

He had left home to begin His sojourn on earth near a manger and stall. Let's get it straight, He was not born in a manger as we often sing at Christmas time. He was born in a stable and laid in a manger. He knew where that manger was and was never lost on earth. He had entered the world of men to obtain a bride, the Church, and when that Bride price of Calvary would be paid, He would then go home to prepare a place for her before coming back for her. Trust Him.

As the disciples watched His ascent to Heaven in Acts 1, two angels of God made it clear that this same Jesus, Who was being taken from them and going up into heaven would return in the exact same manner as they saw Him go. To them it was a new and exciting experience. To Christ, it was an old pathway. He Who had made the worlds and sustained them by the Word of His power, had no trouble on the highway between the worlds. Let alone any problem with the pathways on earth. They were to get about their business of witnessing for His glory. They could trust Him.

When the room is ready, He will return and take us there to be with Him. That truth is so important, that He is coming again, that Paul wrote of it in each of the five chapters of I Thessalonians and then commanded that "this epistle" (which is never said of any other book in the Bible) was to be read to all the brethren. That Christ is coming again is the greatest single truth for believers. Believing in that imminent return will challenge where you go, what you do, and what you say. It will comfort in any trial and fear of life. He may come at any moment. In this particular moment of fear and doubt, trust Him.

We do not know when, but we know Whom. Therefore, we are warned in Matthew 25: 1-13, "Watch." Or warned in the garden as He prayed: "Watch and pray." You can be sure that on the day I sat on Prince at the T in the road, I was wide awake. Only when I knew home was just around the bend did I experience full peace. All my fears were for nothing. I had one who would get me home. Someone I loved and trusted had said so. How much more then should I trust Him Who not only assured me I would make it home, but Himself became the way? It is of no little value that He also said He was the Truth. I can trust Him. Even in the darkest hour or in the greatest fear and time of need, Christ will be there, and He already knows the way.

28 The Unexpected

My old horse was having some problems with seeing, leading to more shying, so the men of the church thought the pastor needed a new, younger horse, and bought one for me! They bought him under good advice, and, best of all, I had known this six year old horse since the hour he had been foaled. I liked his looks: a bright sorrel, three stockings and a sock, and a white blaze. When I saw him now as a six year old, I thought of the old saying when buying horses: One white leg, buy him. Two white legs, try him. Three white legs, shy him. Four white legs and a strip on his nose, knock him in the head and feed him to the crows. I wasn't about to do that. A video had come along with the horse showing how quiet and predictable he was ~ even kids and the ranchers wife were shown riding him. That's why I was so unprepared and surprised.

It was fall, brisk, and he was fat and slick. I warmed him up slowly as we rode from the barn at a walk. After a bit I clucked him into a trot, which I had been taught to do by the former owner. Then, I kissed him into a lope as I had done several times since receiving him as a gift. He took one good step ahead out of the trot, then dropped his head and became completely unglued. I was not expecting it at all and pert near lost the ride. I rode him out, but was so hurt by the initial bucking that I sure walked funny for about three days trying to get my legs where they would be back together and tracking right.

When I went that same week to our 4-H Mounted Drill Team practice, (I was one of the teachers) I noticed that our leader was wearing a back brace and walking like he was on eggs. What happened was that Dave was riding a horse he had owned and ridden often for the past year and a half. As he explained it to me, he was riding, had gone over a mile and a half, and asked his horse for a lope. The horse blew up and Dave was thrown hard. Four ribs were broken. "I just did not expect it," Dave explained. "If I had expected it, I think I could have ridden him." The unexpected. This was constantly true of Christ. He did the unexpected, not to hurt, but to do the will of God. Christ was not God in a box.

In Mark 1:23-27, while teaching in a synagogue, a man who was possessed of an unclean spirit cried out that he knew who Christ was, and questioned if He had come to destroy them. Jesus rebuked the evil spirit, stating: "Be quiet and come out of him." And he did. The parishioners were amazed. What is this? What new doctrine is this? They questioned among themselves. "He commands even the unclean spirits, and they obey Him." How unexpected that was. There is joy in knowing that because Christ has this power over the spirits of Satan, we too can walk in freedom from them. In Revelation 12:11, God makes it clear that we are victors and not victims. We overcome the evil ones by the blood of the Lamb and by the word of our testimony. We speak, resisting them, as Christ spoke, and we are free.

In the second chapter of Mark, verses 5 -12, Christ healed a paralytic by the strange, unexpected words of: "Son, your sins are forgiven you." When questioned as to His authority to forgive sins, He simply used an illustration to answer His own question of which was easier to do, to say "Your sins are forgiven you," or to say, "Arise, take up your bed and walk?" He commanded the man to take up his bed and walk. He did. The question was answered and the people were amazed by the unexpected. Their statement: "We never saw anything like this!" True, God only forgives sins. Christ forgave sins. Christ is God. How wonderful that all of our sins can be forgiven as well. Take them all, whatever they are, to the Christ of the Cross. Hear Him say: "Son/Daughter, your sins are forgiven you." Go then in peace. In going on in Mark, I note chapter 4, verses 35-41. Traveling across the sea, after ministering to the crowds, Christ fell asleep in the boat. A storm arose so furious that the boat was filling with water and the disciples, experienced fishermen, were filling with fear! "Teacher, do You not care that we are perishing?" Yes, He cared, and spoke three words: "Peace, be still." A great calm ensued. The unexpected had taken place causing the men to question: "Who can this be, that even the wind and the sea obey Him?" Who but the Christ, the God Who had made that sea and the wind? He gives us His peace at the moment of redemption, and continues to give peace unlike anything the world can offer.

Did you ever realize how unexpected it was that Christ, that anyone, could walk on water? In Mark 6:47-51, the only logic was that the men were seeing a ghost. Such fear. They were about three and a half to four miles from shore, about three o'clock in the morning, struggling against a fierce wind, and there He was, calmly walking on the water. He calmed their fears by identifying Himself, "It is I, do not be afraid." And then He stepped into the boat, "and the wind ceased." He hadn't said a word to the wind. They were greatly amazed, beyond measure at such an unexpected thing. So today, make sure He is in the boat with you, that's the key to peace in the midst of the storm.

Turning to John, we see one more experience of the unexpected in the life of Christ. Two soldiers had been sent to apprehend Him and bring Him to the temple. [John 7:32, 45-51]. Evidently the crowd was so great that they could not get to Him so had to listen until He was done teaching. Almost like a comedy, they returned to the temple without Him and only seemed to realize it when they were questioned: "Why have you not brought Him?" They had no defense. They had completely neglected their orders. They did have one explanation. The unexpected had happened. It was explained in these words: "No man ever spoke like this Man!" I wish I knew what Christ had taught at that time. Whatever it was, it was so new, so precious, so clear, so challenging that hardened soldiers were moved to the point where they completely forgot why they had attended the meeting. Perhaps, for the first time, life began to make sense for them. I know it did for me when I began to listen to Him.

How often we too try to out-guess, to give directions to God. We don't need to give God orders, we just need to report for duty. He is in control. The joy of adventuring for Christ is that, in Him, throughout all of the journey of life, we can expect the unexpected that always brings glory to Christ and meets the needs of our lives.

29 The Need to Grow

My wife and I were traveling from Pennsylvania to California to be involved in a series of Bible conferences. To be different, and to see the scenery, we took the AMTRAK, and really enjoyed being able to just sit back and watch the country during the daylight hours. As we got deep into Kansas, a sight came to us which we had never expected and could never have guessed. The route took up right past some of the largest cattle feedlots in the nation. In 1972, Texas had the largest feedlot concentration in the nation. This was still true in 1999, with Kansas ranking as the fourth largest. I was interested to see the first feedlot and amazed at the size of it. It seemed to go on for miles. And it did. Then it was followed by other feed lots, again for miles. Feedlots averaging forty to fifty thousand head of cattle. It was almost beyond my ability to believe.

From the Division of Agricultural Sciences and Natural Resources of the Oklahoma State University, and from Oklahoma Cooperative Extension Fact Sheets, I discovered that in 1972 there were 104,340 feedlots in thirteen states, marketing 23.9 million head of cattle. In 1995, in those same thirteen States, there were only 41,365 feedlots, but marketing 23.4 million cattle. By 2002 the ten largest cattle feeding firms owned 53 feedlots with a capacity of six million cattle annually.

Beef is still America's favorite source of protein with the average American eating about 66 pounds annually. A twenty-five million dollar campaign in 1999, encouraged this with the slogan: "Beef, it's what's for dinner."

Millions of farmers, ranchers, business men are deeply interested and involved in the growth and fitting of cattle. God is deeply involved in growth also, the growth in spiritual depth of those who claim to follow His Son, Jesus Christ. In Malachi 4:2, God compares the growth of His followers to the growth of calves: "But unto you that fear My name shall the sun of righteousness arise with healing in His wings; and ye shall go forth, and grow up as calves of the stall." Fattening cattle is not unknown in the Bible. Remember that Abraham had "a tender and good calf" to feed his heavenly visitors. And the father of the prodigal had servants bring forth "the fatted calf" for the party when the prodigal returned. But the growth of the Christian is the burden of God.

Paul spoke in Ephesians four of growing up into a perfect man in Christ. Peter's last words in II Peter three were a plea to grow in the grace and knowledge of Christ – that He might be glorified. John develops the theme as no one else does.

John made it clear in his gospel, chapter 3, verses 3 and 7, that an individual had to be "born again." He must become a baby in Christ. But God will not leave him there. Peter states the one basic truth of all babies: "As newborn babes, desire the sincere milk of the Word, that ye may grow thereby." [I Peter 2:2]. Babies eat a lot and they eat often. If you are truly a newborn child of God's you will be hungry for the Word of God. If you have no desire, no hunger, to be in the Word of God personally, fellowshipping around the word in the house of God with other believers, reading it with your family, you have every right to question if you have been born again. That's the mark of a baby, one who is "born again."

John further develops the growth desired and ordered in his first epistle. He wrote First John for four reasons: (1) That we might have fullness of joy [1:4]; (2) To keep us from sin [2:1]; (3) So we would not be deceived spiritually [2:26]; and (4) To give us assurance of eternal life [5:13]. He also gives us three more stages of the growth of a believer. From the babe who has a hunger for the milk of the Word, John goes on in I John 2:12-14, to describe the stages of little children, fathers, and young men. This is so important to John that he immediately repeats himself to drive his point home.

The little child. No longer a baby. Growing up. [I John 2:12,13]. Scripture reveals that the baby has been forgiven of his sin, what he is. Study Romans 6. I John goes on to deal with the need of the little child to deal with his sins, what he does. "If we say that we have no sin (the sin nature of the unsaved), we deceive ourselves and the truth is not in us." [I John 1:8]. "If we confess our sins (the acts of an individual who is saved, but is growing), He is faithful and just to forgive us our sins and to cleanse us from all unrighteousness." [I John 1:9]. God accepts us into His family as we are, a sinner, but loves us too much to leave us there. He expects us to grow as we are fed. First you get into the Word, then the Word gets into you and change, growth takes place. God longs for holiness in your life.

Fathers. This at first seems out of place when you realize that the last stage is "young men." Seems like Fathers ought to be mentioned last. I argued with God about that for years. What He wants us to know is two-fold. He expects His growing child to reproduce, to have children, to become spiritual fathers. Every saint a soul-winner. There are those to whom you alone can witness, to whom no one else will have access. They are your mission field. Fathers have children. It's as simple as that and every believer ought to have someone they have pointed to Christ. The second truth is that God has no grandchildren. That would follow if "fathers" came last in the list. If you are saved, you are a child of God, not a grandchild.

Young men is the last measure of growth. Above all things else, they have overcome the wicked one, Satan. They are living as victors, not victims. The key of this truth in verse 13 is given in verse 14. They are strong. Why? Because the word of God abides, lives, in them. That's why they have overcome the wicked one. The Psalmist had written: "Thy word have I hid in my heart that I might not sin against Thee." [Psalm 119:11]. The young man is living proof of that Scripture. As a babe he had hungered for and gotten into the Word of God. Growing up, that word had gotten into the very fiber of his life and given him the victory he needed. Fully finished, furnished to know and do the will of God with his life.

You need to grow. Where do you fit in the four stages? How old are you really?

30 Six Lessons from Two Cows

William Shakespeare wrote: "All the world's a stage, and all the men and women merely players." He went on in the poem to express that the life they lived on that stage was in seven roles, finishing in senility. My finding in life is that all of the world is a classroom. We can learn from anyone, everything, at all times. Even the least esteemed person can teach us if we are willing to listen. This is true even of the animals of the world. I was greatly drawn to conviction by the story of two cows in I Samuel, chapter 6.

The background was that Israel was being defeated by the Philistines. So common when Israel was in sin. The elders decided that if the Ark of the Covenant were on the battlefield, victory would be won. Therefore they sent it forth with Hophni and Phinehas, the godless sons of Eli, a priest without discernment or power for holiness.

The arrival of the ark caused great joy for the Israelite soldiers and great fear for the Philistines who stated that "the gods have come into the camp." Their battle cry of "quit you like men" was raised and in an awesome display of might the Ark was captured. Many Israelites were slain, including Hophni and Phinehas. A chain reaction resulted with Eli falling off of a chair by the tabernacle door and dying as the result of a broken neck, which in turn was due to his excessive weight. Phinehas' wife went into labor for childbearing. She died in the process but not before naming the child Ichabod, "the glory has departed." The lot of the victorious Philistines was not altogether pleasant. Mice invaded the land and the capital cities (there were five of them) wherever the Ark was placed. The inhabitants were struck with tumors, and death became a commonality. The people with the leaders panicked. The problem was, they were not sure if these disasters were from the powerful God of Israel or just the circumstances of life. They consulted together and developed a plan to seek the truth of the matter.

First, make a new cart. Second, take two cows which have never been in a yoke; and, which have just freshened, that is, just had calves. Put the calves in a pen. Put the Ark in the cart. In the Ark put some golden images of the tumors and mice as an offering to the God of Israel. Hook up the cows and turn them loose. Cattle are usually considered as dumb, brute beasts. Perhaps this was their thought as they used them. If THEY do what we want them to do, it absolutely would have to be of God. The plot was to see if the cattle would leave their calves, and draw the cart and its contents to the town of Beth Shemesh an Israelite town over the border. If they do so, this is all of God and we've done the right thing. If not, then it was all just chance.

I learned six things from those two cows as they took the Ark of the Covenant back to Israel. First of all, in verses 7 and 10, they were submissive, "hitched to the cart," and no fighting. Humility is one of the greatest things God looks for in an individual. Well has it been said that our greatest ability is our availability. I hear Isaiah saying: "Here am I Lord, send me." Or Paul: "Lord, what would you have me to do?" I can learn submission from a cow.

They were also separated. The calves were "shut up at home." I doubt if they were quiet. In all of the times I have worked at gathering cattle for branding, doctoring, or weaning, I have never gotten used to the bawling that goes on for hours. For days. And even after it quits you can still "hear" it. I imagine two calves were pretty unhappy, but the cows did not look back.

In verse twelve, we read that the cows "headed straight for the road to Beth Shemesh," No deviation, no turning aside, no holding back. They have emotions. They have hearts of love and care for the calves. They went "lowing as they went." But they went. Serving Christ has never been easy. There are heartaches, losses, sorrows. Saints in His service do suffer the same things the world suffers. Sometimes more. We have to answer the question: "Lovest thou Me MORE?" Our straightness on the journey expresses the true love and obedience of our heart. No turning back, no turning back.

They were steadfast. "The cart came into the field of Joshua of Beth Shemesh, and stood there."

That's the way it reads. We understand it was the cows who stood there and the cart did not move. They had finished the course. In Ephesians six we are told to "stand,…withstand…having done all to stand." May we be able to say with Paul: "I have finished the course." What is hindering you right now, from keeping on the course? From finishing it? We can learn from the cows.

Are you willing to be a spectacle in the eyes of the world? These cows were all of that. "When the five lords of the Philistines had seen it, they returned…" Spectacles. Perhaps they thought the cows were weird for they were so unnatural. Surely the world sees us as strange, not running with them to the same excess of sin. We march to a different drum. We follow a different Leader. They watch and they shake their heads.

The final, the sixth lesson, was that they were willing to be a sacrifice. The men of Beth Shemesh "split the wood of the cart and offered the cows as a burnt offering to the Lord." If they had sung instead of lowing, their song might have been: "All, all on the altar laid." Perhaps a Scripture verse for them would have been Romans 12:1, to be a "living sacrifice, wholly, acceptable to the Lord." They were all of that and more. Am I willing to be so? Dumb, brute cows. Were they closer to God, more obedient than I am? Even from them we can learn.

More Resources from Dr. Dale Linebaugh

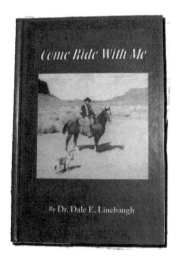

Come Ride with Me

An autobiography of Dr. Dale and Opal Linebaugh, founders of Miracle Mountain Ranch.
Ride with them and learn how God has used the
events in their lives to make them useable and
used for His glory.

To order, contact:
Miracle Mountain Ranch
101 Rodeo Drive
Spring Creek, PA 16436
(814) 664-7673
www.MiracleMountainRanch.org